www.ChildCareExchange.com

Exchange™

The Early Childhood Leaders' Magazine Since 1978

Curriculum:
Art, Music, Movement, Drama

A Beginnings Workshop Book

Edited by Bonnie Neugebauer

CURRICULUM
ART, MUSIC, MOVEMENT, DRAMA

A Beginnings Workshop Book

These articles were collected from the Beginnings Workshop feature of *Exchange —
The Early Childhood Leaders' Magazine*. Every attempt has been made to update information
on authors and other contributors to these articles. We apologize for any biographical
information that is not current.

Exchange is a bimonthly management magazine for directors and owners of early childhood
programs. For more information about *Exchange* and other Exchange publications for
directors and teachers, contact:

Exchange
PO Box 3249
Redmond, WA 98073-3249
(800) 221-2864
www.ChildCareExchange.com

ISBN 0-942702-38-7

Printed in the United States of America

© Exchange Press, Inc., 2006

CURRICULUM
ART, MUSIC, MOVEMENT, DRAMA
A Beginnings Workshop Book

GROSS MOTOR DEVELOPMENT

CREATIVE DRAMATICS

Art

ART

"Look, There is Blue."
A Community of
Artists, Teachers, and Children

by Alison Lutton, Ginny Spade, and Audrey DeCheser

"'Close your eyes,' said Frederick, 'as he climbed on a big stone.' 'Now I send you the rays of the sun. Do you feel how their golden glow . . . .' And as Frederick spoke of the sun, the four little mice began to feel warmer. Was it Frederick's voice? Was it magic?"

If you don't already know Leo Lionni's *Frederick*, the mouse who harvests images and words that will get his family through the winter, then run to the children's section of the nearest library to meet him. Introduce him to your children. Soon Frederick's story will become a part of the culture of your community of children.

Recently Audrey DeCheser's classroom took a walk through the art gallery in Communications Hall, home to the art department on our community college campus. One child sounded a little like Frederick as he drew attention to a particular work of art. "Look," he said. "There is blue."

Most of us read *Frederick* and feel the power we hold to feed or to starve artistic expression in young children. But this story holds a second, equally powerful message for our early childhood programs. This little mouse asks us not just to value and support the artistic development in children but also to reach out to the adult artists in our own communities.

Why you need an art partner

Finding the artists in your community doesn't really take work — it just takes interest. It may mean becoming a local supporter and advocate for the arts. At its best, you will form a real partnership with others who care about the quality of life in your community. You might be surprised at how easily advocacy for the arts and advocacy for early childhood programs can work together.

Our children's centers and associate degree program are home to the Art as a Way of Learning® professional development program. This program encourages arts-integration across the early childhood curriculum, with the help of an art partner. At first exposure, many students think this is not possible. Few programs already have an art partner and many cannot imagine how to get one.

Finding an art partner might begin with something as simple as bringing the authentic work of artists into your classroom. In our program we find that toddlers respond to the bold contrasts and lines of Picasso's *Don Quixote*. This art print displayed near simple black paint and white paper stimulates bold work from two year olds. Preschoolers are often drawn to the brush strokes of Van Gogh's *Starry Night* and to color blocks of Mondrian and Rothko.

The goal in work with any art partner is not to teach children to copy the works of professional artists, but to notice and experiment with age-appropriate art techniques. Toddlers and preschoolers are very interested in experiments with varying brush sizes and strokes, color combinations for mixing, and the effects of paint on varied types of paper. An art print linked to selected materials for exploration can inspire a new idea and give children a connection to the way artists think.

Another beginning point is to think about what you need from an art partner. An art partner is invited into your program as a community artist, not as the art teacher. In partnership, you will support and stimulate each other, respecting each other as experts in your own fields. The artist will form partnerships with the program administrator and with the staff. Over time you will share beliefs about teaching, learning, and the arts. As you plan new ways to integrate the arts into your program, you will share your early childhood expertise, information, and techniques. The artist will share his or her artistic expertise, information, and techniques.

Potential art partners are in every community. You might find yours in a local gallery, a children's theater, a movement or yoga program, or in the art teachers and students at local colleges. Many communities have converted an abandoned factory or warehouse into artist studios open to the public. These community programs often seek community supporters and welcome the opportunity to connect with local educators. Students in our early childhood associate degree program often meet their first arts partner when they work with the art department faculty who teach our Art and Visual Thinking course.

Ginny's story

"The second semester in my early childhood education degree program brought a heightened appreciation for artists and the arts. Pencils were given numbers and density. I developed a feel for the media and creativity that are part of a real art experience. I began to think that I had the ability to bring this process to children. My staff now attend trainings that stimulate art opportunities with new and recycled materials. They bring these ideas back and introduce them to the children.

"My center supplies a multitude of media now as we learn to increase access to art materials in the classroom. This allows the children to build their own ideas, processes, and imaginations. Simple tools and art as a way of teaching can bring out the spirit hiding in the children we serve. Bringing music and dance from different cultures into my classroom transformed the unusually energetic child into a dancer. The ultimate resource would be to bring an artist to the classroom, to touch and feel the artist's spirit."

Ginny's deeper goal was to build a collaborative relationship with an artist who would work with Ginny's child care center for a period of time. As she started to look more deliberately for art partners, they began to appear.

"I recently received a long awaited phone call. For many years I envisioned murals in my center. This day sent me a true gift of partnering. A muralist, Shari, agreed to create murals for my program.

"In my excitement, I spoke to another artist about my good fortune. Ann, a local oil painter, got caught up in this prospect of mural painting. She offered to paint a mural on a portable board for us. My art professor suggested the mural on one side of the board and using the other side to display children's art. This art board could then travel throughout the center and add its special touch wherever it stands.

"Ann also enlightened me about a unique artist-child partnering that already exists in my own community. Artists are recruited to participate in 'Arts Day' held at a nearby school. The artists share oil pastel painting, dancing, bagpipe music, origami, collage making, and watercolors with the children. The eager children spend the day learning many new experiences from generous artists who give this time to share their knowledge. A mountain of wealth can be received when an artist is given the opportunity to share their gifts with children. They bring to the children what they love to do. In enjoying the arts and sharing them, the artists become a resource to children and to the community. The artist's own media builds the bond. Whether pencil or paint, clay or tissue paper, engaging in art with artists will leave an impression and perhaps bring out talent in our youth.

"The arts unite us in so many ways."

The stages of collaboration

As in any collaborative work, an arts partnership tends to develop in stages, a little like children learning to play. The Art as a Way of Learning® program has identified these four stages of arts partnerships.

1

At first, early childhood teachers and artists *coexist* in the same space and time. The early childhood teacher may take the children down the hall to the artist's space, or step aside in her own classroom as the artist takes over. They may watch each other work, but do not yet share information and ideas.

2

In the next stage, the artist and teacher begin to *cooperate*. They begin to share some common short term objectives and to value each other's work. The teacher and artist begin to share information as the teacher learns more about the arts and the artist learns more about young children. The program supports the artist's presence.

3

The third stage, *coordination*, begins when the teacher and the artist begin to adapt to each other. They begin to see a long-term relationship ahead and begin to feel a harmony in their work together.

4

Finally, the teacher and artist begin to *collaborate*. They have built a truly reciprocal relationship based on trust and shared goals. They know each other's work styles and needs. They plan together to design, implement, and sustain projects.

Projects over time support development

One of the benefits of working with an art partner over time is that teachers and children learn about art materials, skills, and techniques. Creative play and exploration are, of course, the goal. But that does not mean that free throwing of paint is the key to artistic development. Artists can teach us about the creative process — nurturing an initial idea, turning it around, playing with it, learning about it. Artists teach us that there is no one right way. One artist develops her work in meticulous thumbnail sketches. Another plays with quick sketches using a lot of movement and revision.

Artists teach us that simple high quality materials offer deeper learning than pre-fabricated activities with "children's materials." Artists can teach us the goal of an art experience. When an artist displays one of Van Gogh's *Sunflower* paintings and then carefully selects paints, brushes, and paper for children, the goal is not to draw sunflowers. It is to explore texture, color, and shape and to help each child learn about the art process, language, and materials. All children don't need to produce or get the same thing from the experience. Sunflower painting may lead to painting the sun. The goal is not to get children to like famous works of art — it is okay for a child to not like a famous painting or piece of music.

For the past few years we have been fortunate to work with Gail Herring, a botanical illustrator who serves as our current artist in residence. She partners with our teachers on curriculum projects, documentation, and displays. "That's the real collaborative part . . . gaining a deep respect for each other and what we each do. Often the learning goals are the same, both want the same thing for children but come at it in different ways."

Artists teach us to have high expectations. Teachers tend to think children cannot do *real art*. Artists help us make the connection to each child's ability to see and represent, to look and to create. Artists help us to see a child's picture or song as a composition with an interesting approach to balance, harmony, or texture. Artists bring a new seriousness to designing and hanging a children's art exhibit.

Audrey's story

"The campus art gallery is one of the stops we make on our daily walk. The children are familiar with looking at and commenting on the art collections. This time the work displayed was textured paper. Most of the children's comments and questions were about the color and the wrinkles." Christin focused on color. 'Look, there is blue.' D'Lanie on texture. 'How come the paper is wrinkled?'"

"When we returned to the classroom, we discussed what we saw, how the paper looked, and imagined how it felt. We don't touch the art at the gallery out of respect for other people's work. I asked the children how we might be able to make wrinkled paper. We decided that squeezing and stepping on paper might work.

"Over the next three days we worked with paper. We submerged brown paper and construction paper of various colors in water. As children squeezed the water out, the paper wrinkled. We put the wet paper on trays to dry in a sunny spot in our hallway. On the third day, we painted on the wrinkled paper. Each day we returned to the art gallery to look at the wrinkle paper exhibit.

"Taking young children out in the community where they can experience things outside of the classroom setting is a rich experience for the teachers as well as the children. Bringing the experience back into the classroom through hands-on exploration provides an environment rich in discovery. To limit what you do because you don't think the children will understand is to disrespect the capabilities of a young child.

"Bringing children to our campus Art Department gallery to view exhibits throughout the year is a learning experience for me as much as it is for them. To witness their sense of wonder and know that we can build on the experience together is awesome. I learn what they would like to do from them. I learn how to do certain types of art right along with them. We have learned together about background, middle ground, and foreground, sequence of work, that a painting can be done in different parts, working over time to create the whole. We have learned a variety of tools and techniques for painting, collage, and sculpture.

"After attending the opening of an exhibit of Outsider Artist's work at a local gallery, I felt a new excitement about art as expression. I felt the excitement of the people who worked so hard to present the artists' work. I began to see my children as outsider artists — community artists without formal training. Each day I wonder where my little outsider artists will take me next."

The halls of our Children's Center were busy this week as Audrey and Gail worked together to create displays documenting our children's visit to the Art Department gallery and their subsequent art work. Children's art pieces, photos, and captions were spread out on the floor as Gail and Audrey considered possible arrangements. Layers of construction paper on the bulletin board created complimentary colors as a background and matting for children's work. The texture of the children's *wrinkle art* pops from the walls. My favorite child quote is Matthew's: "What do you see in this picture, Mrs. D?" He expects his teacher to see and to think like an artist.

Artists and teachers have much in common. We choose our work for its meaning rather than choosing our work to maximize our income, and we have periods of financial crisis. We know that what we do is important to the survival of our community, but we also have periods of uncertainty and deep questions. On our best days we look at our communities and we know what matters. On our best days we can dream something beautiful and express it to others. In partnership, we have much to learn from each other and much to give.

References

Pinciotti, P. (2001). *Art as a Way of Learning®: Explorations in Teaching.* Bethlehem, PA: Northampton Community College.

Lionni, L. (1967). *Frederick.* New York: Alfred A Knopf.

Alison Lutton is an associate professor of Early Childhood Education at Northampton Community College. She is past president of ACCESS, the national association of early childhood teacher educators at associate degree-granting institutions. Alison has worked as a family child care provider, preschool teacher, and in programs for children with disabilities.

Ginny Spade has been a child care center director for 20 years. She is a graduate of the Nursing program and is currently completing a second degree in Early Childhood Education at Northampton Community College.

Audrey DeCheser has been a preschool teacher for 16 years. She is a graduate of the Early Childhood Education program at Northampton Community College. She also has a specialized diploma — Early Childhood Education For Children With Disabilities (NCC).

Using Beginnings Workshop to Train Teachers by Kay Albrecht

A Place to Begin: Lutton recommends the perfect starting place — bringing the authentic work of artists into your classroom. Museum gift shops are great places to begin. They have reprints of famous art pieces in postcard to poster sizes at reasonable prices. To make this a shared experience, plan a field trip to the museum gift shop for teachers to select the artwork that appeals to them. Complete this learning experience by brainstorming ways to use the art examples teachers selected in the classroom.

Experiments Galore!: Your teachers may not be comfortable with working with various brush sizes and strokes, mixing colors, or the effects of paint on various types of paper. Set up an artist studio so they can try them out! Experience is the best teacher; and after experimenting with media, teachers will be more willing to let children do the same.

Four Easy Stages: There they are, on page 8, four easy stages to forming arts partnerships. So, what are you waiting for? Get started by looking for an artist to consider sharing the process with you. Enlist teachers' support to poll parents, family members, and friends to see if anyone can uncover a potential artist in residence to start the process.

ART

Changing Lenses: It's All About Art!

by Patricia Pinciotti

Two days before I am to leave on a US study tour of Reggio Emilia schools my glasses break. Now, I just need them for reading, but I did not want to miss a single moment of this experience. My new glasses became a metaphor for my journey and its connection to my beliefs about children, art, and learning. My encounters with teachers, artists and children, both here and abroad, who understand that *it is all about art* never disappoint me. Their classrooms are filled with inspiring ideas and a bounty of visual and tactile delights. Teachers and children are engaged in careful observations and stimulating dialogue about real learning. In these classrooms, children, parents, teachers, artists, and community members confirm my belief that the early childhood experience is *all about art*. Not art as a noun, a product defined by medium, materials, and size, **but art as a verb**. Art as a verb honors its original meaning and intent, which is to put things together (Booth, 1997).

Here in the United States, our view of art as needing specialized training or our concern with art as something precious or expensive leaves most of us with only an external role in the act of *putting things together*. Most of us approach art as "passive outsiders," ready to be entertained and then critical and disappointed when we are not. We view the art of children as *less than,* cute, or lacking in skills; and unfortunately, what children experience as art and then often what we see is indeed — less than, cute, or lacking content and skills.

Research identifies three different orientations to art in the schools (Bresler, 1993). The *complementary* approach, found most often in early childhood and special needs classrooms, views the arts as self-expression; and therefore anything a child does is considered precious, creative, and worthy. The teacher's role in these classrooms is to supply materials and let children make art. The teacher's involvement in children's art making is supportive; however, the type of artistic guidance or engagement in the process of *putting things together* is very limited.

Another method is identified as *imitative,* approaching the arts as product oriented entertainment. This approach is based on the notion that there is a correct form for art and therefore children's work should look like the example provided by the teacher. Primarily a cut and paste on pre-designed activity, the children and their ability *to put things together* are literally bound by patterns, step-by-step directions, and mediocre examples of a product.

An approach consistent with the work done in arts rich schools such as the preschools of Reggio Emilia and those that take an arts-infused approach to teaching and learning is the *cognitive* approach to art. Here children use art as a language to communicate thoughts, ideas, images, and feelings through various artistic media. Their work demonstrates knowledge of the arts as a discipline, a repertoire of media with artistic reasoning woven throughout the process. In these classrooms children are guided to use art as a way of learning and develop artistic knowledge, skills, and dispositions about visual thinking and ways to put things together (Pinciotti, 2001).

Everyday works of art

A life-affirming view of art, evident in early childhood centers that approach art as a way of learning, is presented by Eric Booth in his book *The Everyday Work of Art* (1997). Booth describes the everyday work of art as the process of making things with meaning, exploring the things others have made, and encountering daily life with a work-of-art attitude. At the heart of the ART experience is the respect and confidence given children as curious learners. These are learners, not unlike artists, who ask questions, explore, compose, and construct with materials and media to understand themselves and their world.

In classrooms where it's all about art, teachers, artists, and parents believe with conviction that this process generates learning both on their part and the children's. They are adamant that children have the minds, hearts, bodies, and hands to explore, hypothesize, test, and make visible a world that is personally meaningful. As Loris Malaguzzi (1990) says, children have a "hundred languages" to grapple with making worlds, exploring worlds, and reading worlds as they construct physical models of their knowing. This is exactly what artists do when they *put things together*, whether with words, their bodies, with voices, or musical instruments, paint, clay, or pencil.

What is it that children do when *it's all about art*, when they are involved in this constructivist approach to making meaning with words, bodies, voices, instruments, and artists' tools? We know from research that students who attend "high arts" schools are able to do certain things better than students who attend "low arts" schools (*Champions of Change*, 1999). That somehow making *it all about art* does something to how students think and act as they individually or collectively *put things together*.

Expressing ideas and feelings openly and thoughtfully

We are beings of communication. From our very first entry into the world we scan faces for responses. We learn to cry and coo various ways to convey different feelings and desires. The significant adults in our lives learn to read and understand our sounds, movements, thinking, and feeling. How can children continue to communicate their emerging quantity of complex ideas and feelings if they are not given multiple languages to communicate well? How can they *put things together* for someone to understand if they are required to use only words or numbers?

Describe a spiral staircase or a helicopter just using words? Impossible! Significant involvement in the arts provides a repertoire of tools to communicate ideas and feelings openly and thoughtfully. Artistic choices are made so these ideas and feelings are expressed with care. We know learning is impeded in the absence of personal interest. Schools where learning is infused with the arts have higher attendance rates and less vandalism (Fowler, 1994). An environment where children are required *to put things together* mentally and physically gives them reasons to come to school, reasons to exist. Maybe it's all about art.

Layering and forming relationships among different items of experience

We know from research on the brain that the search for meaning is innate and this searching occurs through patterning. The arts offer a direct path to seeking patterns, layering experiences, and making meaning. Meaningful learning engages feelings,

experiences, relationships, and the ability to see clearly with our eyes, hands, and bodies.

Children become problem posers in art-rich environments. They call on their personal life of images and experiences to solve problems. The answer to the question, "What color is this?" or "How does this animal move?" is not moment specific, but tied to their whole life as a learner in the world. Ask someone who has experimented with color, who knows how color mixes and interacts with other colors, someone who has multiple images for the color "orange." Check with someone who has watched ants at work for a long time, or has been caught off guard by a cat leaping from the floor to a table, someone who has run or spun around really, really fast. Becoming better readers and writers, understanding numbers, forming successful personal relationships involves *putting many things together*, layering experiences to solve word, number, or people problems. So maybe it's all about art?

Imagining different vantage points and working towards a resolution

Art is messy! Recall your last attempt to *put something together* — a great dinner, a bicycle, your early childhood portfolio, or your taxes. Didn't it get messy first before it made sense, before it came together? The problem-solving path is not always straight — clean — clear — neat. Children in high arts programs are able to see or imagine things from different vantage points. Working in the arts, children come to know that the same steps, notes, or colors may lead to dramatically different results depending on their individual vision.

The arts are essentially about diversity. Art is about you and me and how we see both similarly and differently. Whether I am working *to put things together* to show you what I see from my perspective, or how you and I have to work collaboratively *to put things together*, the arts always value differences. In dance or drama, we must share and negotiate our individual perspectives to create one idea together, working toward a consensual solution. Consensual means the joining of the senses to agree together on a perspective and a direction. When one works in the arts he or she truly appreciates individual efforts. Even as young artists, children know different is good. Real art is always about communicating and sharing how we see the world collectively and uniquely. Maybe it's all about art?

Constructing and organizing thoughts and ideas into meaningful units

Frank Wilson in his book, *The Hand* (1998), puts forth a radical idea about cognition. He believes that the work of the hand leads the mind. Constructing occurs not only in your head, but also through your hands and body to develop your mind.

Constructing and organizing — *putting things together* — physically is at the heart of mind making. Through art explorations the eye, the hand, and body work together to create the mind. What are children's hands doing in your classroom? How much time do bodies sit? The hand — thought — language — culture are inextricably connected. Through the physical medium of the arts, whether it is clay, voice, paint, movement, paper, or wood, children construct and share meaning in a social environment. What if it is what you do with your hands that creates your mind? How do children use their hands to know their world — *to put things together* — to make meaning, to create something that they value and share with others. The brain has the capacity for language, but the body is the tool of language. Learning through the hands and body is what is remembered, constructed, and organized. Maybe it is all about art?

Children from high arts schools are able to focus perceptions on an aspect of an experience and sustain this focus over a period of time. Sustained perceptions! Not rushing — giving time for learning. The arts need and use time to awaken the senses, to relaunch an idea, or to focus perceptions over time. One of the things the arts do is slow down time (Sylwester, 1995). We have all had one of those "zone" or "right brain" experiences. Maybe it happened as you began rearranging your classroom, your exercise routine, or working in your garden, when you lost track of time. When was the last time the art of reawakening your senses took over and you gave yourself up to a sustained perception?

Real learning engages the entire physiology — the senses, hands, mind, and body. The arts by their very nature involve engagement — focused perceptions. One of the complaints of classroom teachers is that doing art takes so much time, particularly in this world of academics and high stakes testing.

Maybe this is why the arts are essential for learning, to balance the one answer with in-depth learning in and through time. Take time with your children. Make your classrooms a real learning place, a place for wonder, curiosity, and perceptual awareness, a place where children have time to construct, to make a mess, to organize, and *put things together*. And ultimately be learners in the act of creating themselves! Maybe it is all about art?

As early childhood educators we believe that children are resourceful, curious, and competent, with a relentless desire to interact and communicate with others. Challenge yourself to break set and "see" with an artist's eye and embrace a culture of teaching and learning that values and believes in the work of the hands in the act of *putting it together*. What if the work we do is all about art? What do you need to learn today to set the stage for artistic learning in your classroom? What would that mean for children and our view of teaching and learning if everything we did was all about art?

References

Booth, E. (1997) *The everyday work of art: How artistic experience can transform your life.* Naperville, IL: Sourcebooks, Inc.

Bresler. L. (1993). "Three orientations of arts in the primary grades: Implications for curriculum reform." *Arts Education Policy Review, 94*(6). 29-34.

Champions of Change: The impact of the arts on learning. (1999). http://www.aep-arts.org

Fowler, C., (1994). "Strong Arts, Strong Schools." *Educational Leadership, 2*(5). 4-9.

Malaguzzi, L. (1990). Poem. (Written as an introduction to the European exhibition "The Hundred Languages of Children.")

Pinciotti, P. with Berry, D., Sterman, C., & Gorton, R. L. (2001). *Art as a Way of Learning: Explorations in Teaching.* Bethlehem, PA: Northampton Community College.

Sylwester, R. (1995). *A celebration of neurons: An educator's guide to the human brain.* Alexandria, VA: ASCD.

Wilson, F. (1998). *The hand: How its use shapes the brain, language, and human culture.* New York: Vintage Books.

Patricia Pinciotti, Ed. D. is chair of the Early Childhood and Elementary Education department at East Stroudsburg University in eastern Pennsylvania. She is a teacher, artist, author, speaker, and mother of three who tries to make every day a work of art.

Using Beginnings Workshop to Train Teachers by Kay Albrecht

Which one describes your program?: Pinciotti reports three different orientations to art in schools. Convene teachers to explore which one describes your program and whether orientation is what they really want. If not, explore the steps to change it, using the articles in this issue of Beginnings Workshop as a study tool.

Do you have the conviction?: The author reports that classrooms where it is all about the arts have parents and teachers who believe that process generates learning. Do your teachers have this conviction? Do parents and other family members? If not, explore why and what you might do to share your convictions!

The work of the hand leads the mind: Explore with teachers the wonderful questions posed about hands and how children use them to construct what they know about the world. Analyze your curriculum to make sure children's hands are creating, constructing, and putting it together every day.

ART

Art for All Children:
A Conversation About Inclusion

by Nancie Tonner West

*Conversation is the way we discover
how to transform our world, together.*
— Margaret Wheatley

The value of conversation

Maria organizes her notes as she prepares to join KidTalk, a time set aside for teachers' conversation about children. Today, a special educator and therapist will help the teachers prepare for welcoming Peter, a child identified with special needs. Maria has several questions she wants to explore and looks forward to exchanging some ideas that may be useful in planning appropriate art experiences for the new child.

A regularly scheduled conversation about including all children of differing abilities in art experiences provides teachers with time for reflection on child learning. Our discussions focus on ways we can support children as they engage in thinking, talking, and creating. During this time we analyze and interpret our observations and ask specific questions that draw upon the experience of each person engaged in supporting the child (Jones, 1986). It is in dialogue with each other and as a group that we create a shared framework for working together. As we listen, explore our questions, share our ideas and feelings we reflect the image of ourselves as teacher learners. (Rinaldi, 2001). These intentional conversations build the foundation necessary to ensure children of differing abilities benefit from art experiences.

Try this:
■ Engage in "intentional talks" about inclusion of all children in art experiences.
■ Discuss observations of what children do with materials, what they say and teachers' hypotheses of what children might be thinking.
■ Develop thoughtful questions to guide discussion.

Conversation about children with differing abilities

Maria is observing children's investigations at the light table. During a recent trip to the teacher supply store, Maria discovered translucent round shapes used for mathematic counters in the primary grades. Peter has joined the children turning the glasses upside down. The children alternate mirrors and glasses, rearranging the multi-colored counters. Peter follows their lead and adds three counters to the design, remaining engaged for several minutes. Maria reviews Peter's individualized education goals. She wonders if there is a way she can incorporate his interest in organizing "things we see through." She plans to discuss her ideas with her director.

We all want to feel welcomed, to belong and be accepted in our family, our neighborhood, and by our peers. Being a part of a community is the right of all children. If we are to create a welcoming early education community for all children including those with special needs, we must ask ourselves some difficult questions: What is my bias? What stereotypes influence us and interfere with our belief in the competence of every child? According to Carla Rinaldi (2001), "Dealing with differences is difficult and requires commitment and hard work." Sandy Peterson, author of *When Children Soar With the Wind: Including Children with Special Needs* (2004), affirms this when she writes, "Our attitudes and beliefs about disability may be invisible to us, and yet they will determine our decisions and actions toward children with disabilities."

Try this:
■ Reflect on the feelings and attitudes we bring to inclusion.
■ Examine the language used to describe or discuss a child with differing abilities and avoid out-dated or pejorative words.

Create a culture affirming the value of diversity

Maria has brought in a box of glass beads from Africa. The children select beads to examine and the group talks about their characteristics. Lorene has a limited vocabulary and communicates with gestures. She places the beads in a line on the table. Cyrus, Jackson, and Libby invent complex designs on swatches of fabric. Maria offers the suggestion: "You can draw your designs and I will take photographs." The children comment as they review the photographs and drawings. Although Lorene does not draw her design, she enjoys seeing pictures and hearing the description of her "bead story." Maria shares this story at KidTalk. With the assistance of the special education consultant, teachers explore ideas to build on Lorene's strengths.

The concept of universal design — the design of experiences and environments to allow all people participation without the need for adaptation or specialized design — guides Maria's art planning. Utilizing these principles can make programs more welcoming to children with special needs and decrease the need for specialized equipment. We do this by choosing, adapting, and using everyday materials in ways that enhance children's opportunities to participate, play, and learn (Haugen, 2005).

In the preceding illustration Maria relies on her knowledge of children's artistic development to appropriately modify her responses to the age and stage of each child (Goldhawk, 1998). Lorene's behavior is typical of the way an older toddler approaches materials; she is enchanted with one aspect of action — standing the beads up. Maria celebrates the unique expressions and learning process of each child. Similarly, Ellen Daniels, a special educator in Conifer, Colorado, describes the many ways that art experiences enhance children's development:

- Painting at the easel promotes gross motor development of the upper body.
- Drawing, clay, and bead stringing develop fine motor and pre-writing skills.
- Talking about art and the art process encourages speech and language development.
- Engagement in visual art stimulates cognitive learning.
- Children learn cooperative skills when working together on an art project.

Try this:
- Introduce children to new experiences through guided exploration.
- Demonstrate how to use art tools and provide explanations of art media.
- Adapt or modify your responses, expectations, and language to match the developmental age and stage of each child.
- Allow children daily uninterrupted blocks of time for art experiences.

- Support children's desire to revisit a media or endeavor for many days, weeks.
- When adaptive tools and equipment are necessary, seek out designs that appeal to all children (i.e., brushes with round handles).
- Deepen your understanding of children with differing abilities.
- Evaluate the art space: look at organization; accessibility; attractiveness; reflections of children and adults of differing ability.

Conversation about art for all children

When children visit the art area the next day, Maria introduces the term "sculpture" and invites the children to create lines in space with wire and beads. The children twist their designs into various snake-like shapes as they string translucent beads. Peter holds the wire between his fingers flipping it back and forth. Adam recalls how he attached Styrofoam® with toothpicks and Maria encourages Adam to pursue this idea. Adam sticks the wire into the Styrofoam® pieces. He forms a mental picture of a "train" and selects several pieces for the cars. Jackson initiates a construction with the same materials, naming it a front loader. Peter is interested in the Styrofoam® and breaks it into small sections. Maria encourages Adam and Jackson to work together on a group project and invites Peter to contribute his collection of Styrofoam® to this endeavor. "We discovered many ways to use our materials today," says Maria. Maria engages the children in talking about how their art is the same and different. The group generates a list to share during community time.

We can think of art as an integrated component of all children's educational experiences. What are the outcomes for *all* children when we include children with differing abilities in art experiences? How do art experiences develop an appreciation for diversity? How can art activities be designed to allow children to participate without the need for specialized equipment?

Ursula Kolbe, author of *Rapunzel's Supermarket — All About Young Children and Their Art* (2001), describes the development of children's social understanding when she writes, "As children listen to other's ideas and see each other's work, they have opportunities to learn that there are different points of view." Young children continually categorize, arrange, match, and transform the objects and materials in their environment. According to Deb Curtis and Margie Carter (2003), children have a natural eye for design and "can make good use of diverse, attractively displayed open-ended materials. As they explore textures, shapes, colors, and sizes, they notice how things are alike and how they are different." Teachers and special education staff at the Arvada West Preschool in Colorado maintain, "Children learn they can show the world who they are inside and what they are thinking, even though they can't say it in words. We need to believe in and be comfortable with all children exploring materials and experiencing art in their own way whether through total immersion or simply touching the materials."

Try this:
- Help children discover the ways their art and art process is similar and different.
- Facilitate open-ended art experiences with potential for variation and discovery.
- Build on children's interests when planning art experiences.
- Promote **inquiry,** problem solving, and creative thinking.
- Encourage children to talk and **collaborate** together on group projects doing sculpture, murals, weaving, printmaking, **and clay work.**
- Offer invitations to create with natural and found materials (Curtis, 2004; Weisman & Gandini, 1999).

Conversation on art education

Maria explains the changes in her thinking about art. "When I first started teaching, I was not creative. I gave children shapes for pasting to resemble the model I prepared. Then I attended workshops and learned ways to provide children with open-ended art experiences. I was still frustrated because so much of their work looked 'ugly' or did not have meaning. An art specialist offered suggestions and helped me think about the value of art experiences for young children. This exchange increased my confidence. Now that I know more about art, I feel better prepared to respond to children with differing abilities."

Through ongoing conversation we can challenge our assumptions about art, artists, and art education and redefine our practice.

- How important are art experiences for young children?
- What is our purpose in offering art to young children?
- What do children learn from art experiences?
- What are the roles of an art specialist, special educator, and therapist and how can they help us in our work?
- Can we provide a meaningful art program if we do not have training in art education and do not feel creative?
- How do we move from teacher-directed art activities to facilitating meaningful art experiences planned in collaboration with children?
- How can we engage parents in our arts partnership?
- What community resources can support us in our work?

Through art we:
- Experience the joy of creating ("making and doing")
- Represent ideas and feelings using the "language of art"
- Develop creative and critical thinking ability
- Reflect on our learning and our thinking
- Collaborate with others to solve problems
- Invent unique products
- Decode visual communication

- Enjoy the qualities of materials
- Explore art processes
- Appreciate the art of artists and peers
- See the value of difference
- Understand how we are the same
- Learn math and literacy concepts
- Form a disposition for artistic experience**s**

Dewey (1956) believed that construction with art materials ("built up" work) draws upon the child's natural motivation to explore materials. The process of constructing develops observation skills and sharpens the senses. Art experiences increase children's personal responsibility for their work, which emerges through many actions and decisions.

Try this:
- Write and display a statement about the value of art for all children.
- Document observations of children and use the information for planning art experiences and guiding the teaching process.
- Exhibit art by children and artists including art by individuals with differing abilities.
- Invite artists with differing abilities to talk with children.
- Read children's books about art and artists with and without disabilities.
- Do your own art with different media, and reflect on the creative process.
- Encourage representing through drawing, sculpture, and other art "languages" as part of science and project investigations.
- Become familiar with national, state, and local art standards.

Conversation on collaboration

Angela talks with Maria about her hopes and dreams for her daughter Tenisha. "I would like you to assume she is competent and encourage her to participate even if it is only for fleeting moments. It takes extra effort to engage her. She enjoys physical movement such as getting her hands and feet into the paint and messing around. I would like you to meet her where she is developmentally. Most important, I want Tenisha to learn how to be with other children."

Jonathan describes his son to Maria. "Michael started drawing before age two. He covered the kitchen floor, refrigerator, and even the washing machine with drawings. Michael has many challenges and uses art as an outlet to express himself. The fine motor action helps him close off what he sees as the chaos of the world. When he goes into his world of drawing he feels a semblance of control over his world. Drawing brings beauty to his life."

Partnerships with parents of children with differing abilities are necessary to achieve the goal of successful inclusionary art experiences and may include the following questions:

- What do you see as important outcomes for your child?
- What special education goals can we support through art?
- How does your child feel about "getting messy"?
- What modifications (if any) do you make for your child?
- Will the specialists supporting your child provide staff training or technical assistance?
- Does the child have any health or other needs that impact his participation in art activities?
- What do you see as our role in your child's art experience?

Successful collaboration requires time and the commitment to ongoing conversation and planning, opportunities to learn from specialists, discuss what has worked, and develop our understanding of each child's needs and growth.

Try this:
- Commit to collaboration between staff, parents, art specialists, special educators, and, therapists.
- Seek out community, state, and national resources for training and technical assistance.

Conclusion

Adequate support is necessary to make inclusive environments work. In addition to conversation, support includes training, planning time, and ongoing consultation with specialists (Schwartz, Odom, & Sandall, 1999). Our journey towards successful inclusion of all young children in art involves:

- Constructing meaningful art curriculum with children
- Scaffolding learning for children with differing abilities
- Matching art experiences to individualized education plans
- Learning different art media and processes, and
- Adapting activities to the age and stage of individual children

Communication among adults paves the way for effective collaboration among teachers, parents, and the support team. Ongoing dialogue in a collegial atmosphere forms the foundation for ensuring all children with differing abilities in our programs experience the wonder and joy of art.

References

Curtis, D., & Carter, M. (2003) *Designs for living and learning: Transforming early childhood environments.* St. Paul, MN: RedLeaf Press.

Curtis, D. (2004, May/June). "Environments to engage children." *Exchange, 157,* 38-40.

Dewey, J. (1956). *The child and the curriculum and the school and society.* Chicago: The University of Chicago Press.

Goldhawk, S., & The Task Force on Children's Learning and the Arts: Birth to Age Eight. (1998). *Making creative connections.* Washington, DC: Arts Education Partnership.

Haugen, K. (2005). "Learning materials for children of all abilities." *Exchange,* Out of the Box Training Kits.

Jones, E. (1986). *Teaching adults: An active learning approach.* Washington, DC: NAEYC.

Kolbe, U. (2001). *Rapunzel's supermarket: All about young children and their art.* Paddington, Australia: Peppinot Press.

Peterson, S. (2004). "When children soar with the wind: Including children with special needs." In Colorado Department of Education Early Childhood Initiatives *Expanding quality in infant toddler care curriculum,* pp. 1-28. Denver, CO: Colorado Department of Education.

Rinaldi, C. (2001). "Documentation and assessment: What is the relationship?" In Project Zero; Reggio Children, pp. 78-89. *Making learning visible: Children as individual and group learners.* Cambridge, MA: Reggio Children.

Rinaldi, C. (2001). "Infant-toddler centers and preschools as places of culture." In Project Zero: Reggio Children, pp. 38-47. *Making learning visible: Children as individual and group learners.* Cambridge, MA: Reggio Children.

Schwartz, I., Odom, S., & Sandall, S. (1999, November). "Including young children with special needs." *Exchange, 130,* 74-78.

Wheatley, M. J. (2002*). Turning to one another: Simple conversations to restore hope to the future.* San Francisco, CA: Berrett-Koehler Publishers, Inc.

Weisman C. T., & Gandini, L. (1999). *Beautiful stuff: Learning with found materials.* Worcester, MA: Davis Publications, Inc.

Resources

- **Circle of Inclusion**: www.circleofinclusion.org

- **Child Care plus+:** http://ruralinstitute.umt.edu/childcareplus

- **Educational Resources Information Center (ERIC) Clearinghouse on Elementary and Early Childhood Education:** http://ericeece.org

- **National Association for Education of Young Children (NAEYC):** www.naeyc.org

- **National Child Care Information Center:** http://nccic.org

■ **National Head Start Disabilities Services Training Center:** http://ccf.edc.org//ntcl

■ **Special Education Resources on the Internet (SERI):** http://seriweb.com

■ **The Council for Exceptional Children (CEC):** www.cec.sped.org

■ **Very Special Arts:** www.VSA.org

■ **VSA** *Start with the Arts Curriculum.* www.VSA.org

■ **Zero to Three: National Center for Infants, Toddlers and Families:** www.zerotothree.org

---

Nancie Tonner West, M.S., stimulates learning through art with children and adults in various settings including early education programs and art centers. She is an instructor and coach for the Colorado Expanding Quality for Infants and Toddlers initiative at Family Resources and Child Care Education, Red Rocks Community College. West received her B.A. degree in art education from Montclair University, New Jersey, and M.S. degree in Supervision and Administration from the Bank Street College Early Education Leadership Program. She has coordinated and directed early education inclusion programs and conducts seminars on the creative process involved in art experiences. West credits her appreciation of human diversity to her childhood experiences with Peter, a sibling with developmental disabilities who continues to amaze and delight her.

Using Beginnings Workshop to Train Teachers by Kay Albrecht

Do you believe in conversation?: What a wonderful question! Find out if your teachers believe using the three suggestions listed on page 15.

Creating a culture affirming the value of diversity: Try the list on page 16 to tackle the challenge to create a culture that affirms the value of diversity.

Conversations about art of all children: Challenged to find ways to include all children in art activities? Discuss the suggestions on page 17 with teachers and make plans to implement the ones that each teacher finds most intriguing.

Worth doing: Challenge your teachers' assumptions about art, artists, and art education by asking teachers to individually answer the questions posed on page 17. Then, convene small groups to share and discuss their responses. End with action planning to redefine practices.

Extend the conversation: West's conversation on collaboration could easily be expanded beyond art experiences to other kinds of experiences in your school. Extend the conversation by tackling other types of learning experiences children have in your program.

Library resources: The great list of printed and Internet resources provides a perfect starting place. Identify two or three teachers who are willing to see what they can find that might be worth adding to the program's professional library.

Art Experiences

ART EXPERIENCES

Educationally Appropriate Art Activities for Young Children

by Bernard Spodek

The arts have long played an important role in early childhood programs. Unfortunately, too often art activities are not educational — that is, children do not learn nor do they learn about art from them. While early childhood activities need to be developmentally appropriate, they also need to be educationally appropriate.

Art activities that are educationally appropriate can serve two purposes:

■ They can help children better understand the world in which they live.

■ They can help children learn about the nature of art.

Art activities can contribute to children's capacity to make and understand meaning (Smith, 1982). Art creations stand for objects, feelings, or ideas. In symbolizing their world in art, children actively engage in making sense of their world. This is seen in the work of the Reggio Emilia preschools in Italy (New, 1990). The schools offer project-like activities where children use their own observations to collect information about various aspects of the world around them. They work with art educators to symbolize their observations. Their art activities help these children to gain meaning from their experiences and to order and express these meanings. Their products are also artistic.

Art is one of the symbolic tools of a culture; language is another. As young children talk about their drawings and read their marks, they describe the meanings in their drawings. Later, children use language to regulate their drawings — planning them as well as their play activities. In this way, children's drawings are linked to speech. The symbolic activity of creating art gives way to the symbolic activity of telling stories, and later writing them (Dyson, 1993).

Using early childhood artwork to help children understand their world can be found in other places as well. Similar activities have been found in programs in New Zealand, in the English infant schools that practiced the "integrated day," and in an approach to education called "Open Education." They probably also occur in many contemporary American preschools. In all these programs, the work of young children — their drawings, paintings or clay works, their dances or dramatic productions — are valued both as works of art and as vehicles by which children come to understand their world.

Young children can also be helped to become artists and to understand art. They can develop the symbolic tools of literacy in the visual arts, "reading" the aesthetic symbols of their culture (Davis and Gardner, 1993). This is done in programs for older children called "disciplined based art education." The discipline of art can be a basis for early childhood programs as well. We can develop activities that not only help young children produce art, but also learn about art history, aesthetics, and art criticism.

Building on children's intuitive knowledge and their potential for making observations, teachers can help children become aware of the qualities of their artwork. They can surround children with mature art. Teachers can also provide children with tools for art and help them become more competent in their control of those tools. These elements can be provided in a way that is developmentally appropriate. By using the foundation of the discipline of art, the activities can also be educationally worthwhile.

Exploring the discipline of art in early childhood education

Discipline based art education consists of four components: (1) art production; (2) art history; (3) art criticism; and (4) aesthetics. Let me discuss each of these separately.

Art production. Most of the art activities we do with young children are related to art production. The product itself should not be the goal of the activity; rather, the activities should help children develop competency in the use of art media. They should allow children to express their ideas and feelings with deliberateness and planning, so that what is completed is what was intended, though children's artwork may also change as the result of the child's being stimulated by the process itself.

It might be best to focus in the beginning on a limited number of media with very young children, such as paint, clay, crayons, and markers. These materials can be controlled easily so that children express themselves well. Children also become more competent with these materials the more they use them. Helping young children become more competent allows them to truly become artistic.

Art history. Children below the primary grades lack the understanding of time to understand formal history. However, they can learn informal history when it is presented in a concrete manner. Art history should be presented to young children in a concrete form.

A good example of such concrete presentations is found in the *Early Childhood Discovery Boxes* of the Toledo Museum of Art. Each Discovery Box includes a teacher's guide, a set of art reproductions, some costumes and props, books, an audio cassette tape, and other resources. Using these materials, the children learn about the time and culture related to the works of art.

Many local art museums or children's museums have similar materials available or provide similar activities. Most museums welcome groups of young children, and the staff of the museum can help you develop activities to use in your center.

Art criticism. Art criticism involves children in provocative art dialogues as they view a work of art (Cole & Schaefer, 1990). Art criticism activities can be organized into four stages. In the first stage, *description*, the children are asked to list all the visible qualities of a work of art. Exploring the relationships between these qualities (line, shape, color, texture, and balance) is the stage of *analysis*. In the third stage, *interpretation*, the children focus on ideas, feelings, or moods expressed by the artwork. In the final stage, a *judgment* is made about the artwork based on information previously discussed.

Museum reproductions of art could be kept in the classroom for several weeks so that children can go through these stages with the same piece of art. Books of art, such as the *Come Look With Me* series by Gladys S. Blizzard (Charlottesville, VA: Thommasson-Grant), can also be used. This series of four books — *Enjoying Art with Children, Exploring Landscape Art with Children, Animals in Art,* and *World of Play* — contain reproductions of art from many periods. Each picture is accompanied by information about the content of the picture as well as questions that can be asked about the picture.

You can also use the artwork that children create themselves as a basis for criticism. This form of criticism is not telling a child whether his product is good or not. Rather, it is concerned with helping children learn to make thoughtful observation a process that they can engage in on a day-to-day basis as they review their own work.

Aesthetics. There are many ways in which we can make children more sensitive to the beauty that surrounds them and help them understand the aesthetic elements in their culture. This requires that we surround the children with things that are beautiful and make the school setting more aesthetically pleasing.

An example of this can be found in traditional Japanese homes and inns which contain a *tokonoma*. This is an alcove that is devoted to the display of something beautiful — a scroll, a flower arrangement, or a ceramic piece, for example. The display adds beauty to the surroundings. You often see such a beauty area in Japanese kindergartens as well.

You could establish your own *tokonoma*, or beauty display area, in your room, just as you might have a science or nature display area. An art reproduction or a vase of flowers could be tastefully displayed in this area. You could change the display regularly. Each time a new display is put up, it would help to discuss the display with the children: Why do we consider it beautiful? What do the children like about it?

You could also display the children's artwork in special ways. A few pictures — possibly simply framed — could be displayed carefully on a special section of a wall, or the children's clay work could be displayed in your own tokonoma. A piece of cloth draped over a box or large block makes an attractive pedestal for children's clay work.

Art postcards or small reproductions of works of art can be purchased in museums or gift shops. Children can match identical reproductions to one another. Later, the reproductions could be paired to similar paintings by the same artist, and later to group paintings by artist. Using this approach, children could learn to appreciate a range of artworks as well as learn about artists and their times (Wolf, 1990).

The children might even try working in the style of distinctive artists. Thickening paint with cornstarch and providing vivid colors could allow children to paint in the style of Van Gogh. Providing interesting shapes could allow children to make collages in the style of Dubuffet. This would be an interesting extension of their becoming more sensitive to the works of particular artists.

Art, like language, is a way of symbolizing knowledge. Our culture provides us with the symbolic tool of discourse — the spoken and written language that allows us to make and communicate meanings to others. It provides us with nondiscursive symbolic tools as well — including pictures, movement, and music — that allow us to make and communicate meanings. Sometimes meanings that cannot be expressed well in words can be well expressed in these other symbolic forms. All these forms of making and sharing meaning are interrelated. Giving children linguistic tools of language literacy helps children deal with and communicate ideas and feelings. So does giving them the symbolic tools of the arts. All symbol systems help children deal with ideas and feelings and help make them better thinkers and learners. By building on the discipline of art, teachers can provide another way to empower young children.

References

Cole, E., & Schaefer., C. (1990). "Can Young Children Be Art Critics?" *Young Children*, 45(2), 33-38.

Davis, J., & Gardner, H. (1993). "The Arts and Early Childhood Education: A Cognitive Developmental Portrait of the Young Child As Artist. In B. Spodek (editor), *Handbook of Research on the Education of Young Children*. New York: Macmillan, 1993.

Dyson, A. H. (1993). "From Prop to Mediator: The Changing Role of Written Language in Children's Symbolic Repertoire. In B. Spodek and O. N. Saracho (editors), *Language and Literacy in Early Childhood Education. Yearbook in Early Childhood Education, Volume 4*. New York: Teachers College Press.

New, R. (1990). "Excellent Early Education: A City in Italy Has It." *Young Children*, 45(6), 4-10.

Smith, N. R. (1982). "The Visual Arts in Early Childhood Education: Development and Creation of Meaning." In B. Spodek (editor), *Handbook of Research in Early Childhood Education*. New York: Free Press.

Wolf, A. D. (1990). "Art Postcards — Another Aspect of Your Aesthetics Program?" *Young Children*, 45(2), 39-43.

I would like to thank Oliva N. Saracho for her suggestions.

Bernard Spodek is Professor Emeritus of Early Childhood Education at the University of Illinois, where he taught since 1965. He received his doctorate from Teachers College, Columbia University. His research and scholarly interests are in the areas of curriculum, teaching, and teacher education in early childhood education. Dr. Spodek's most recent books include *International Perspectives on Research in Early Childhood Education*, the latest in the series *Contemporary Perspectives in Early Childhood Education*, all edited by Olivia N. Saracho and Bernard Spodek and published by Information Age Publishing, and the 2nd edition of the *Handbook of Research on the Educaiton of Young Children*, edited with Olivia Saracho and published by Erlbaum. He is also president of the Pacific Early Childhood Education Research Association.

ART EXPERIENCES

Teachers and Children Together: Constructing New Learning

by Lella Gandini

A story

We find two teachers intent on placing on a large table many samples of different papers they had been collecting. They are trying to divide them according to weight from lightest to heaviest.

Now they realize that it is difficult to ignore the differences in color, which gets in the way of their first attempt to categorize by weight. As a solution, they decide to work at first just with white paper.

Immediately, as they proceed to touch and handle their selections, they notice how the pieces of white paper — tissue, rice paper, parchment, tracing paper, typing paper, newsprint, packing paper — are distinct and differ not only in weight, of course, but also in texture, pliability, and feel. As they move them around, some seem to catch the breeze, while others remain flat and rigid. "Look, they also have different ways to show the light if you hold the pieces up to it." Now they start to place the white papers on the windowpanes. "Oh, look at the shadow of that tree on the paper; it's working as a screen."

This selection and exploration takes a long time and gives much pleasure. The teachers learn about the properties of paper in general and of those different pieces that are making an attractive design on the table. Paper has become more and more a material full of surprises. The two teachers, as they continue to work, realize that tearing and crumpling paper makes interesting sounds, that collages can have an infinite palette of colors and textures, and that adding the design of letters and words and cut-out images opens up many possibilities for beautiful pictures and intense narratives.

Later, they start a list of verbs that communicate the different actions that working with paper implies, such as crumpling, folding, tearing, cutting, gluing. . . .

At a certain point, they stop to reflect about their experience. They go over the sequence of their decisions to learn more about the possibilities of paper as a material to use with the young children in their classroom.

They had given themselves the following tasks:

■ We will look independently for as much variety of paper samples as we can find.

■ We will make notes about where we found each kind of paper, about its availability, size, weight (and eventually cost).

■ We will collect it neatly in a box, and then we will meet and we will surprise each other with what we found.

■ Together, we will divide the paper in categories; we will experiment and make a list of what could be done with each or with the combination of various kinds of paper.

Now, thinking back, they reflect: "Are we learning all these secrets to teach them directly to our children? We gave ourselves trust and time, and we gave ourselves a chance to pursue unknown paths in order to make discoveries. We should offer the children the same chance. But we have also learned a great deal from our experience; now we can offer a good selection of paper, and we know how to display it to enhance specific aspects. We helped each other with our uncertainties, with our questions, and with what we learned; now we can support children with questions and offer them skills when they need them. Other discoveries and other questions will be suggested by the children themselves, and together with them we will continue to learn about this."

Materials can be used to enhance the learning experience of young children (and their teachers) by opening new avenues for discovering, creating, and constructing. There are many materials that have that potential all around us; they can be brought inside the classroom together with the usual crayons, markers, scissors, paper, and glue. And even the variety and the use of crayons, markers, scissors, paper, and glue can be expanded and transformed into a powerful mine of ideas, as our first story tells us.

It is helpful to look around and observe what is available or search for things that can be used, combined, or transformed. It is not obvious or easy at first — but when we start to pay attention, our eyes gradually will see better and detect more paths to potential materials that our environment offers for our work and pleasure.

If we go on a walk in the woods, we will begin to see interesting leaves, twigs, chips of bark, acorns, pine cones, grasses. Let us just observe the leaves we found. How can we put side by side combining or contrasting shape, size, colors, texture, the fresh and the dried ones? Is the skeleton visible or not? From what tree do they come?

If we are near a beach or a river, we could find shells, pebbles, or splinters of wood bleached by the sun. What about on the environment closer to our daily chores, like a supermarket? Let us look at the variety of fruit displayed there. Could we take some to school to observe, touch, cut open, and taste? Could we keep the peel to dry and use for our collages? Could we explore the seeds of these fruits, plant them, and keep track to see if they sprout and how?

Another story

A teacher in a classroom of five year olds decided to try out clay with the children. She thought the children could shape a small bowl to give to their parents as a gift. There was a kiln available in the school; therefore, she thought, the bowls could be fired and then painted.

When I visited the classroom, this teacher was disappointed and frustrated. The children had not become involved as she hoped; they had hurriedly shaped approximate, tentative bowls; and now that it was time to paint them, they did so with a few dabs of color and rushed back to other things available in the room. "I guess these children are not artistically inclined when it comes to clay, or else I am not able to give life to this experience" was her comment.

We turned to look at the children who had left the table with the abandoned, sad bowls. Some of those children were building with blocks. I noticed right away how complex the block structure was and how eagerly the children were adding and modifying parts, discussing and negotiating the next steps in their building within the group.

The teacher saw my interest, smiled, and with enthusiasm began to explain: the children were working on the cityscape, and they had discussed with her some of the buildings they knew. As their interest grew, they had decided together to place the silhouette drawing of the city skyline behind the block area. They had discussed the problems of building bridges and highways and had made drawings as plans. They had selected the different shapes of blocks to make ramps and had become aware of the fact that small blocks placed together became as big as the larger blocks.

As she went on, her narrative and her observations about the children's discoveries and learning showed competence and pleasure. At a certain point, she stopped to breathe, and I asked: "Do you like clay?" She was surprised, but just for a few seconds. "I see," she said, "You noticed how much I like blocks. I realize I know very little about clay and its properties; I feel a little uneasy about it; and I never used it myself. I wanted to give the children an artistic experience, and now you help me realize the difference in the way I approached this experience and the one with blocks." The experience of that teacher and those children working with blocks had been a co-construction; their learning was constructed together.

It happens often that the continuous availability, abundance, and variety of blocks — as well as of special space set-ups and of time available for block play, plus the extended experience of teachers with that material — make block play into a very developed, constructive, and creative language. Other materials, that is, other potential languages, have less space, time, and variety. Often teachers have not had a chance to observe or experiment with them; therefore, there is less attention given to the way they are offered to children.

Another problem frequently encountered is the notion that *art* or *art activities* are something separate from the learning experiences of children; the same is true of the thought than an exploration of harmony and beauty can be done only with a limited range of materials, called *art materials*, only in a specific corner of the classroom, and only at a set time of day. There is also a tendency to think that an experience for children, in order to be creative and *artistic*, can only be spontaneous, open ended, and perhaps messy.

The fear of focusing too much on the product rather than the process makes teachers afraid to offer the children the chance to improve and feel successful and pleased with what they want to make. To give that possibility to children requires offering them occasions to learn skills at the moment they feel that they need them, or when it is clear that without them they could get stuck or become discouraged. What is called for is that delicate and observant way of being with children, sustaining them, and encouraging them to go forward when they are about ready to do so. To construct new learning with them is a way to respect their potential. And, by the way, they do not need to be considered artists; that is an adult notion.

Co-exploration of materials in Reggio Emilia

We turn to the schools of Reggio Emilia to reflect with those teachers on ways to support the explorations of very young children with materials in such a way that those explorations become meaningful experiences. The educators here feel that it is useful to be close to the children, especially when they begin to explore new materials, in order to sustain their discovery and to enjoy it with them, but also to open the way to constructing communication through the materials.

The teachers strongly believe that children desire to learn and have potentially many ways to communicate their feelings, their interests, and their questions about themselves and the world around them. The goal of the teachers is to give, gradually and remaining respectful of the children's own time, a repertoire of many media and materials. These media and materials they consider to be languages because they make communication possible and open the door to learning.

With that in mind, the teachers organize the space of the classroom in such a way that many engaging activities that children can do by themselves are available. Several of these are set up so that children can gather in small, autonomous groups. When a new material or a new project is presented to one group, one of the teachers will stay with that group while the other will be available to the rest of the children.

When children are three or younger, the range of materials should be presented gradually, but the occasions to explore and construct with them should be many. These occasions become part of the ongoing daily activities, to create continuity and familiarity, while at the same time offering the pleasure of discovering and being surprised.

There are many different materials that are developmentally appropriate for very young children. Some of the materials we have seen in the Reggio infant-toddler centers or schools are familiar to all of us, but the teachers, working together, have found ways to extend and enrich some apparently simple objects.

We saw baskets with pieces of cloth, large enough to cover the head of a child if she/he wants to dress up or to play peek-a-boo, but not too large to become difficult to handle. Those were cloth remnants creating a palette of color, texture, and even transparency. Paper and cardboard make wonderfully versatile materials, so do water and food coloring to pour and mix in transparent plastic containers. We know well the power of non-toxic paint of many brilliant colors to use with different kinds of paper and with different sizes of brushes. But we also saw soft, pliable wire of various thickness for shaping into different forms (and telling good stories), along with other malleable materials such as clay. Clay is used a great deal in large or small quantities for opening up worlds of exploration, pleasure, and learning.

Let us look more closely at a beginning exploration of clay.

A third story

A teacher is sitting at a small table with four three year old children. In the middle of the table is a large piece of clay. She has worked the clay in advance to make it manageably soft. As the children reach out to grab pieces of clay and make comments to themselves or the others, the teacher observes them and takes notes on a pad. Watching their glee, she asks one of them how the clay feels. Then she turns to another child and says: "Marina says the clay is cold, what do you think?" "Not cold, it is wet and squishy." The other children laugh and repeat "squishy, squishy." They squeeze the clay, they pound on it, and they flatten it, making sounds and talking.

The teacher observes a child beginning to make a snake and attracts the attention of the others to what he is doing. "That is great. What are you doing, Luca?" Luca giggles: "A long thing!" He rolls the snake quickly, and the snake breaks. "Broken!" Luca is perplexed. The teacher: "Try again; let us find out why it broke up" and to the other children who now are watching Luca intently: "Do you want to try? How did Luca move his hands to do that snake?" They all go back to work. Luca is more careful and the snake does not break right away.

The others experiment with some success. But Elena has a hard time; she is close to tears. The teacher gets up, goes close to her, lowers herself to her side, and puts her arms around her to guide her hands. "If you do not press too much, you can feel the clay inside your hands, inside your palms. See? It is getting round and rolling." She accompanies Elena's hand a few times but in a lighter and lighter way. She stays close without touching her. Elena is now making progress and smiling. The teacher goes back to sit at the side of the table and to take notes. Soon the children are called to lunch. She shows them how to cover the clay and their work with a wet cloth. Everything, however, remains available for later.

It is the following day when the same children go back to the table. The teacher reminds them about what they had done and points to the snakes. "Do you want to try more? What could we make with them?" The children are eager to do more and as they work they come up with different sizes and combinations of snakes. They tell stories or give descriptions of what they are doing.

The teacher takes photographs of the children working, getting details of their clay forms; today, she has a tape recorder to capture their words. She asks them questions and takes notes. At times, she also makes quick sketches of the children's constructions. All of these observations will be shared with her co-teacher and the other teachers in the school. All together, they will discuss both the experience and ways to further it as well as offer it to the other children. This is how teachers in Reggio keep track of the children's experiences and deepen their own understandings. But they will also put together documentation through a notebook, a panel, or a letter to parents. They want the parents to feel part of the life of their children in the school and want to communicate to them (and to the children as well) not only what the children are doing but also how and why.

Teachers, children, and parents working together with materials: this is part of an approach where learning is valued, considered reciprocal, and constructed as a shared process.

Resource

Edwards, C., L. Gandini, and G. Forman (editors). *The Hundred Languages of Children*. Norwood, NJ: Ablex Press, 1993.

Lella Gandini, M.A. from Smith College, and Ed.D. from the University of Massachusetts, Amherst, was Adjunct Professor in the School of Education at the University of Massachusetts, Amherst. She has carried out comparative research projects on teaching of young children and on parent-teacher-child relationships in Tuscany, Emilia-Romagna, and in New England. She works with teachers of young children in various municipalities in Italy, among them Pistoia and Reggio Emilia. For Reggio Children she serves as liaison for the dissemination of the Reggio Emilia approach in the United States. She conducts professional development, lectures frequently, and has published several articles and book chapters about the Reggio Emilia approach to early education. She produced, with George Forman, videos presenting and examining projects in the schools of Reggio Emilia, including "An Amusement Park for Birds." With Carolyn Edwards and George Forman she co-edited and contributed to the book *The Hundred Languages of Children: The Reggio Emilia Approach to Early Childhood Education*, first edition 1993 and the second edition in 1998 with the subtitle *Advanced Reflections*. In 1999 with Cathy Weisman Topal, *Beautiful Stuff! Learning with Found Materials*, Davis Publications, Inc. In 2001 with Carolyn Edwards, *Bambini: The Italian Approach to Infant/Toddler Care*, and in 2005 with Lynn Hill, Louise Cadwell, and Chuck Schwall *In the Spirit of the Studio: Learning from the Atelier of Reggio Emilia.*

ART EXPERIENCES

Fostering Experiences Between Young Children and Clay

by Cathy Weisman Topal

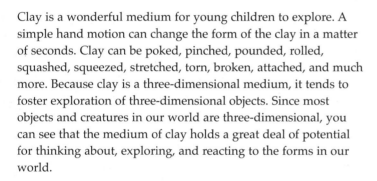

Clay is a wonderful medium for young children to explore. A simple hand motion can change the form of the clay in a matter of seconds. Clay can be poked, pinched, pounded, rolled, squashed, squeezed, stretched, torn, broken, attached, and much more. Because clay is a three-dimensional medium, it tends to foster exploration of three-dimensional objects. Since most objects and creatures in our world are three-dimensional, you can see that the medium of clay holds a great deal of potential for thinking about, exploring, and reacting to the forms in our world.

Clay is therapeutic. When one works with clay, a special kind of communication takes place between the hands, the clay, and the imagination. It is a very personal experience. Clay is responsive. It gives immediate feedback. Anyone can make a shape in clay and, with experience, gain more skill and control in shaping clay into a desired form.

Generally, young children approach clay by squeezing, pressing, and pounding it with their hands and fingers. They become familiar with the feel of the clay. As children spend more time with clay, they gain control over their hand movements and begin to construct with the clay. They discover that they can break pieces of clay apart and form balls and coils. They begin to find form in their work and often talk to themselves as they manipulate the clay. You might hear stories of snakes, mountains, monsters, and caves, even though the clay may look like a big lump to you. In essence, the above stages of working with clay correspond to the scribbling stages in drawing. Uncontrolled pounding and pressing become more controlled balls, coils, and shapes which the child then names and arranges in various design configurations. Paralleling the design stage, the child finds that he or she can shape clay to resemble realistic forms and scenarios.

If clay is such a wonderful medium, why isn't it more widely used? Most teachers would say that they don't use it because it

is messy or that they haven't had any experience with clay themselves. In actuality, once a teacher has a bag of clay, a few work boards, and a knowledge of basic clay skills, clay is an easy material to pull out anytime and to put away.

Introducing clay

In our introductory discussion, I want to generate a feeling of wonder and appreciation about this natural material that comes from the earth — that actually is earth. I want children to have a sense that it is a basic medium that people have shaped in countless ways since the beginning of time.

As I ask questions, I am constantly manipulating the clay, suggesting possibilities, and pushing it back into a lump. It is important that children see their teacher enjoying the feel of the clay as she explores it. Sometimes I'll read excerpts from *When Clay Sings* by Byrd Baylor which I think helps children to appreciate the material that they are about to use:

. . . Now Indian children make a game of searching for bits of clay that were once somebody's bowl or mug or cooking pot or dipper. . . . They say that every piece of clay is a piece of someone's life. . . . They say the clay remembers the hands that made it. . . .

I always introduce clay by asking the following questions to see what ideas the children already have. "Does anyone know what this is?" Yes, clay. It's different from play dough which we make from flour. After you have worked with the clay a little bit, see if you can figure out some differences. (Clay is firmer. It can be built taller, encourages more intricate work, and holds it shape much better than play dough. Working with clay leads to very different and more in-depth experiences. But working with play dough is a good introduction to using three-dimensional, malleable materials.)

"Do you have any idea where clay comes from?" Clay comes from the earth. It is made up of fine-grained particles of rock that are broken down over many years and then are mixed with mater. The color of the clay depends on the particular rocks and minerals. Clay is usually found near water. "Has anyone ever dug clay from the ground?"

"Can you think of any things that are made from clay?" (flower pots, plates, bowls, cups, sculptures, bricks, even houses)

Exploratory exercises — Exercises for warming up hands, clay, and imaginations

Children need time to get used to the feel of the clay. The following exercises are simply ideas for guiding exploration. As you watch and listen to the children, you will have a few strategies ready for picking up on what children are already doing, and you will have a sense of which exploration to introduce next. Each exercise calls different muscles of the hands, fingers, and arms into play and encourages the development of a variety of different kinds of hand control and skill in using clay. Each kind of hand movement tends to tap certain associative and imaginative experiences. *Hands are the only essential tools.* Refrain from giving out sticks and other implements which remove the hands from the clay and from the manipulative experience. A fist size ball of clay is a good beginning size.

1. **Discover at least two ways that your hands can change the shape of the clay and tell me what you discover.** Can you poke it? Pinch it? Squash it? Flatten it? Squeeze it? Start keeping a record of the descriptive words that children use as a reference. Descriptive words increase children's vocabularies and are a means of helping children revisit an experience. "Roby found that he could use his thumbs to poke deep holes into the clay." "Sarah likes using her fingers to smooth the clay." "Molly pressed and flattened her clay to make big, thin pancakes which she rolled and stood up."

2. **Shaking hands with clay.** Children naturally begin making clay pancakes, so why not capitalize on that tendency and actually explore the different parts of the hand and the different lines and textures that they can make. Explore how they can change the texture and surface of the clay.

■ Pat your clay into a large pancake and cover it with fingerprints. Cover the entire surface. Close your eyes. Feel the surface of your clay. What does it feel like — bumpy or smooth? Turn your clay over. Try knuckle prints — remember to cover the entire surface. Does this texture feel different than the fingerprints? How? Try thumb prints, palms, fists, elbows, fingernails, and the side of your hand. Can you guess which part of the hand made a particular impression?

■ Make a finger texture chart. What kind of textures can you make by just using your fingers? Try poking shallow holes and deep holes, pinching small ridges, pulling long grooves, alternating thumb prints. Children can choose one of their finger textures for the chart. It should be different from the ones already collected and it must cover the entire pancake. Children should be able to say how theirs is different. You might help by pointing out differences in size, depth, and direction.

■ Poke space into your clay by poking places that go in and through. Make big and little indentations. Can you make a see-through place? Turn your clay around and look at it from different points of view. Try it next to a light source and look at the shadows.

3. **Squeezing tall shapes with clay.** Many children do not engage their arm and shoulder muscles while they work with clay or with other materials. It is actually many of these same muscles that are necessary for the development of writing skills in the future.

The following exercises are ways to encourage children to begin using these muscles during play and exploration. Let children know that it is important for them to use these muscles, and that you will help them to see if they are using them by gently laying your hands on their shoulders. You'll be able to feel the movement, and so will the children.

These exercises require a bit more clay. Working from a big soft lump of clay in the middle of the table and encouraging children to pull clay from the lump, shape it, and reattach it is another option for this exercise. It tends to encourage group work. Again, demonstrating as you talk is very important.

■ Can you push, squeeze, and shape your clay into a tall mountain? How high can you squeeze your shape before it begins to droop? Use your fingers, knuckles, and thumbs to make textures, holes, tunnels, and caves. Can you connect your clay with a friend's to make a mountain range?

■ Pinching and pulling places that come out. Identify pinching fingers. Try modeling or pinching the air before moving to the clay. Go around each protuberance lightly with your first finger and thumb to strengthen. Make your protuberances thick and sturdy.

■ Pinching/pulling/modeling a ridge. This is another hand strengthening skill and a way to make a strong protuberance. Encourage children to use all of their hand muscles, not just the fingertips. Can you feel the difference? Try pulling up a strong and tall ridge or fence.

■ Sharing your discoveries. Children love to share their discoveries and to talk about their work. In fact, stepping back and taking a look at what has happened is an easy and exciting way of generating new enthusiasm, as well as new ideas and techniques. You will be surprised at the depth of children's thinking, vocabularies, and perceptions.

When I see that children have created some interesting structures, or that attention is waning, I'll stop the children and ask them to go around the table and share *one* discovery that they made about clay. Or I might ask them to tell what part of their hand they used to shape a particular part of the clay and what kind of movement they used. This sharing time always gives children new ideas. Sometimes I'll say, "Now go back and try out one idea that interests you from our sharing session."

At other times, I'll give clean-up instructions: "Put your clay back into a ball. Use your clay as a stamp to collect all the tiny bits of clay on the table. Now poke a deep hole with your thumb. I'll pour some water into it and you can close it up. The water will work itself into the clay so that it will be soft enough to use tomorrow."

■ Squeeze and sculpt. Squeezed shapes are often suggestive of fantastic creatures and dinosaurs. After a few sessions of exploration and squeezing, children have a great time making squeeze creatures. Reading books such as *Goodnight, Dear Monster* by Terry Nell Morris and *Where the Wild Things Are* by Maurice Sendak gives ideas for parts of creatures to include.

Name all the many parts of a creature first — head, body, legs, tail, eyes, nose, mouth, horns, toes, scales, wings, whiskers. Start by squeezing a sturdy and interesting shape. Turn it around to find the head. Poke a mouth. Pull legs, tail, and wings. Add on coils and balls for eyes, nose, ears, teeth and press them on.

4. **Breaking clay into pieces** and reassembling in a new way is another focus to use to explore clay.

■ Rolling coils generally precedes rolling balls and is an exciting and rewarding clay skill to practice. Take a small piece of clay and roll it back and forth between your hands. When it is too big to hold, put it down on the table and roll it back and forth between two hands. Keep your hands moving gently over the clay. Practice to see how much pressure you need. Standing up and using the weight of your body makes rolling coils easier. Closing eyes makes your fingers even more sensitive. It helps your fingers know where they need to go. Try making fat coils and thin coils, long coils and short coils. Join coils together. Roll some into spirals. Stand some coils up in the air.

Step back and try to record the children's thinking, conversations, and observations. Here are a few remarks made by a small group of three year olds practicing rolling coils: "I'm making a whole lot of circles." "I made a ring. I really made an 'O' instead of a ring." "I made a person. Lookit — a snake! I'm making a lot of legs for this person because it's a spider person — a lot of legs — 1, 2, 3, 4, 5, 6 legs. See?" "I made a person. I made a kind of dinosaur that nobody knows what it is." "I made an egg on toast." "Do you know how I made these (marks on clay)? With my fingernails!"

■ Rolling balls. Balls can be rolled between your hands or on the table. Which method works best for you? Can you roll tiny balls between the tips of your finger and thumb? To roll a ball, hands need to move around and around, whereas rolling a coil or snake demands rolling back and forth and back and forth. Instead of telling the children, let them discover and articulate the difference in their own words. Try to record what they say.

■ Rolling balls and coils. After practicing rolling balls and coils for a day or two, try this exercise on a separate day. Be sure to refer to the skills and descriptive words that the children have been using. "Emily discovered that she could make a circle from her coil. Kristi made a family of snakes, Joe put all of his coils together to make a dinosaur. Camille rolled her coil into a spiral." Break a ball of clay into at least six pieces. Roll at least three coils and three balls — more if you like. Then put them together in a new way. You'll be surprised at what children construct. Design configurations, animals, spiders, people, forts, and bridges are popular constructions. Group constructions are also fun.

■ Drawing your construction. One of the first ideas that I tried after returning from a trip to several pre-primary schools in Reggio Emilia was to ask children to draw what they constructed. The first time I tried this with four year olds, I was scared that I was asking them to do something that was too difficult. I was amazed. They did it easily. I was intrigued and began asking children to draw constructions that they had made in other materials as well. When children began saying "Can I draw it now?," I knew something important was happening.

As an alternative to saving work, try asking children to draw their construction just as they built it, starting with the first shape, or the bottom. They can select the point of view that they find most interesting or that they like best. I like to give children black fine line markers to use because of their clarity. This causes them to think back over the experience and the various steps of their construction process.

5. **Constructing with balls, coils, and slabs.** The exploratory exercises listed above are also ways of practicing basic clay skills. When children can form and describe how to make coils, balls, pancakes or slabs, and squeezed shapes, they are ready to use clay to construct something that interests them.

The key to constructing or recreating what you know about a form, such as a face or person or classroom pet, is to explore it by touching it (if that is possible) and to identify and name the parts. You can ask children which part they will start with and which method (balls, coils, etc.) they will use to make that part. It is the reverse of finding form in the shapes that the clay suggests.

Using rolled forms makes the parts distinct and easy to *read* visually.

6. A few tips about using clay.

■ Purchasing clay. Clay can be purchased in most local art stores and from potters living in your area. Look up pottery making supplies in your telephone book. Try to get moist, low fire red, gray, buff, or white clay that is ready for use. Clay is relatively inexpensive and can be used over and over again before it is fired in a kiln. It is not necessary to save most clay experiments, but occasionally there may be something you do want to save.

Clay sculptures can simply be left to air dry or they can be fired in a kiln. There are also several oven-fire clays on the market that can be baked in an oven at about 250 degrees Fahrenheit. There are self-hardening clays as well. Often there are parents who are potters or who have had experiences with clay and would welcome the chance to help introduce clay.

■ Work surfaces. Children can work directly on a table but, for the long term, I prefer small pieces of 1/8" thick treated Masonite about 10" square as a resting place for clay and a way to carry it around. Cardboard squares also work. Covering the table with a large garbage bag taped to the bottom of the table is another alternative. Children can simply return all the clay to the middle, and you can wrap it up in the bag for storage.

■ Consistency of clay. Before distributing clay, wedge it a little bit (like kneading bread) to be sure it is an even and workable consistency. I have found that children may not want to touch the clay if it is too wet and sticky or too hard. If the clay is too wet, spread it out on a board for a little while, then wedge it. If it is too hard, break it apart into small pieces, put it in a plastic bag, add water, and let it sit for a few days. Then wedge it. Learning about the properties of clay can be another

way to explore clay. If the clay seems too hard one day, that is a good day to practice squeezing water into the clay as well as smoothing with water.

■ Storing clay. Clay must be kept in an air-tight container. If children wish to continue working on something that they have already begun, simply cover the clay and work board with a plastic bag and seal with a twist.

As you think about bringing clay into your classroom, remember to emphasize exploration using a variety of different approaches. Introduce one or two provocations at a time to generate interest and excitement. When interest begins to wane, pick up on something that one of the children is trying to introduce a new way to think about exploring clay. It is during the exploratory process that ideas, vocabulary, clay skills, and control develop. Recording children's thinking, and reading their words back to them, and encouraging them to draw their configurations leads to more interesting and in-depth work.

NOTE: Many parts of this article were taken from Cathy Weisman Topal's book, *Children, Clay and Sculpture* (Worcester, MA: Davis Publications, Inc., 1983). Other sections are excerpts from a forthcoming book, also from Davis Publications, on materials in the early childhood classroom. The author reserves the right to reproduce parts of this article.

References

Baylor, B. (illustrated by Tom Bahti). (1981). *When Clay Sings*. New York: Atheneum (an Aladdin Book).

Brown, E. V. (December 1986). "A Critical Need: Children and Clay." *School Arts*, 12-13.

Kellogg, R. (1969). *Analyzing Children's Art*. Mountain View, CA: Mayfield Publishing Company.

Silberstein-Storfer, M. (with Mablen Jones). (1982). *Doing Art Together*. New York: The Metropolitan Museum of Art.

Speight, C. F. (1979). *Hands in Clay*. Sherman Oaks, CA: Alfred Publishing Company, Inc..

Topal, C. W. (1983). *Children, Clay and Sculpture*. Worcester, MA: Davis Publications, Inc.

Cathy Weisman Topal has been an art teacher for over 25 years and currently teaches three- to eight-year-old children at the Smith College Campus School in Northampton, Massachusetts. She also teaches visual arts education at Smith College. Cathy is the author of four art resource books, *Children, Clay and Sculpture; Children and Painting; Beautiful Stuff: Learning with Found Materials* (which was co-authored with Lella Gandini); and *Thinking with a Line*, a multimedia computer program and a Teacher's Guide. All of the above were published by Davis Publications, Inc. of Worcester, Massachusetts. For more information please visit Cathy's web site for Thinking with a Line: www.smith.edu/twal.

ART EXPERIENCES

Negotiating with Art Media to Deepen Learning

by George Forman

Art is an interpretation of experience, not a high fidelity copy. Art causes us to look at how we look at something. Art calls attention to itself. Therefore, at a minimum, an appropriate art activity even for young children encourages children to look at how they look, to treat their art as an expression of their current understanding rather than a representation of an object. This perspective makes art a rather paradoxical enterprise, a planned journey into the unknown, a negotiation with the tools for making meaning. And art media are just that — tools to help children make their ideas visible, their thoughts, theories, and perspectives, and in the process traverse the terrain of their own bias in order to construct a new understanding of the subject.

Children learn a great deal when they use several media to express the same idea. They begin to understand that each type of representation captures different aspects of their concept. When children routinely cycle a single concept by rendering it with different media, they begin to understand that each rendering is just that, a first draft of their idea, a perspective that they take when working in a particular medium, to be rethought when the concept is rendered in the next medium.

Using several media to deepen learning

An object drawn with markers will look different when made in stiff paper and wire. For example, the volcano a child drew in our preschool had a huge red ball of fire on top of a brown cone with a flat top. The wire and paper volcano had a great empty volume and a sense of pent-up power. The drawing portrayed the immense size of the lava; the paper and wire volcano represented the mass and slope of the mountain down which the lava would flow. These representations were both attempts to represent (and we should say re-invent) the volcano. Together, they deepened the child's understanding of the volcano.

When the teacher revisited the drawing with the child, she asked him about the rather perfect circle of fire (an unlikely configuration for exploding lava). She also asked him about the flat top of the volcano because this flat top was made only on his volcanoes, not on other hills that he drew. He explained that there was lava all around this big rock (instead of lava being hot rock). Thus we can understand why he drew the red lava in a spherical shape, given that a big boulder would have this look. He explained further that the volcanoes have a hole, thus the flat top. The lava splashes out when the rock falls into the hole and hits the lava. The idea that the *splash* comes from an eruption of released pressure was not prominent in his mind.

When the teacher revisited the paper and wire volcano, the discussion turned more to where the lava would fall. Would it all be near the top? Children, looking at the paper and wire model, began to think about lava rolling down the sides of this three dimensional mass and spewing out and falling all around the base of the model. We decided to pop popcorn through the opening of the paper and wire volcano so the children could test their ideas about where the *lava* would fall.

Certainly the children profited from rendering volcanoes both with graphic markers and with paper and wire sculpture. The drawings allowed the children to express their theory about the lava itself, how it looks coming out and how it moves as it explodes. But the paper and wire model helped the children think more clearly about the interface between the lava and the mountain, how it flows down the side and eventually how the lava itself makes the mountain grow. Their knowledge deepened as they integrated what they learned from each medium. The drawings on paper, in effect, represent questions that can be answered as children traffic through different media.

Different media allow different expressions

Drawings allow the children to represent most any idea. The marks need not conform to the constraints of the physical world, e.g., the pull of gravity, the actual shape of a working part, the transitory presence of a movement. This freedom to make even their implausible ideas visible helps children later when they attempt to understand more completely. They have a record of their theories and this visible public record helps them negotiate deeper meaning with others.

Wire and paper models allow children to compare the drawn theories with what might actually work. The wire and paper model directs the children's thoughts to the kinetic aspects of the volcano, the flow of the lava down the physical surface of the model. The voluminous sculpture also directs their thoughts to what is happening inside, an aspect less salient in the drawing.Each medium orients children to different aspects of the subject matter. Each medium makes certain questions more *askable* than other questions. And in order to eventually find the solution to any problem, children have to ask of the event many different types of questions. Thus by using a variety of media to represent a single phenomenon, we are helping children ask better questions.

Blocks help children ask questions about the balance (both gravitational and visual) because the elements of this medium are easily moved as modules and because the elements actually fall when physical laws are violated.

Clay helps children ask questions about the gradual transformation of one shape into another, something impossible with blocks. Thus clay would be a good medium if we wanted children to consider the four or five stages in a growth process or the procedure by which a geological formation was made.

String helps children ask questions about boundaries and continuities, particularly when these lines need to be changed in small ways from time to time. With string, the *line* can be modified slightly rather than having to redraw an entire pencil mark. This medium encourages the children to consider not only how the boundary changed but also how the boundary remained the same. Thinking about change within invariance is fundamental to a deeper understanding of natural phenomenon.

The importance of cross comparisons

It is important to ask children to compare their representation in medium one with their representation in medium two. In the case of the volcano, the children should bring their drawings to the studio where the wire and paper model was made. As was said before, the drawings often present assumptions about the phenomenon that might be clarified in the second medium.

The children talk about both the drawing and the paper and wire model in a deliberate attempt to reconcile their differences or to use one to answer questions raised by the other. The teacher can set this up as follows: "Jason, I notice that in your drawing the volcano has a flat top. Where is that in our model?" While this is a simple question, almost rhetorical, it holds the potential of having Jason begin to describe his theory about the splashing lava, but this time in the presence of the wire and paper model. Talking about this theory in front of the wire and paper model could help Jason reconstruct his theory, specifically because the paper and wire model will more likely cause him to think about elements erupting from the inside rather than being thrown in from the outside.

The importance of redoing the first representation

The traffic through different medium should not be treated as a linear progression, say from two dimensional first then on to three dimensional media, or from a written script to the acted play. Traffic needs to flow in a cycle where children return to the first representation. Drawings are redone after sculpting, scripts are rewritten after being tested on the stage. It is in the reconstruction of the first representation that true learning occurs, where new knowledge is integrated into the initial knowledge, where new knowledge reveals the gaps in the initial version. It is the understanding of errors, not their avoidance, that defines meaningful learning.

In the case of our volcano activity, we could ask Jason to look at his first drawing, the one where the lava was drawn as a large red sphere. How would he modify this drawing after modeling it in wire and paper? He may choose to capture the flow of lava down the mountain and that in turn might cause him to reconsider the lava as a liquid state rather than a solid state. It is interesting to note that in the presence of the model his talk was all about the tiny streams of lava that flow down the *cracks* in the mountain. It is important for us to help Jason confront his ideas about liquid states and solid states by revisiting and redoing his initial drawing. This editing and doing again is a step often omitted in today's classrooms. Without this step, we run the risk of having new knowledge exist without challenging the initial theories, theories that sometimes are held more strongly by deeply felt, but incorrect, intuitions.

Art as a tool for thinking

Art can help us look at how we look at life. When children use a variety of media to represent their current view of something, we can help them realize that these representations do not say the same thing. We do this by cross comparisons among the media and by encouraging children to redo their work within each medium. In this manner, art becomes a tool for thinking. Children draw to learn as opposed to merely learn to draw. Children are revising their theories, not simply revising the accuracy of a copy. In this regard, art becomes part of the core curriculum.

Resource

Forman, G. (1989). "Helping Children Ask Good Questions." In B. Neugebauer (editor), *The Wonder of It: Exploring How the World Works*. Redmond, WA: Exchange Press.

George Forman is an emeritus professor at the University of Massachusetts School of Education at Amherst, Massachusetts. Dr. Forman is a well known author of books that extend the developmental theory of Jean Piaget to early childhood education. He has also published books in the areas of early symbolic development and the educational value of digital technology. Dr. Forman has created video documentaries in the preprimary schools of Reggio Emilia in Italy to bring their educational model (a coherent approach that integrates art and symbolization as a means to educate children from three to six years of age) to prominence in the United States. He is currently president of Videatives, Inc., a company that produces web based digital video resources for teachers to help them see what children know and how children think.

Music and Movement

MUSIC AND MOVEMENT

For the Love of Music — and Children

by Cindy Smith

Music increases the joy in our program at Holy Trinity Preschool. The children at Holy Trinity experience how much fun it is to make music together! Music doesn't just happen in our "music room" with the "music teacher." It happens throughout the preschool, all morning long. Music happens in every classroom. You can hear teachers and children singing songs during group times and transitioning times, during pick-up and hand-washing times, and of course during our designated "music time" in our "music room."

Three days out of five I get to teach music classes for two- to five-year-old children. Five out of five days I am also the director of preschool ministries at Holy Trinity Lutheran Preschool in Littleton, Colorado. What a joy and privilege it is to be able to step out of my office and step into the "music room," where children have gathered (sitting on the floor) and are anxiously awaiting to do what comes so naturally to them, and that is to make music.

Making music helps children express their feelings, boosts early language skills, enhances their self-esteem, and soothes their souls. It allows children to investigate rhythm, become aware of their bodies, and explore other cultures.

Making music with children is easy and fun! You do not have to be a highly trained musician to enjoy and share music with young children. I have a secret I will dare to share. I am not a highly trained musician. I cannot play the piano or any other instrument for that matter. What I have is a love for music and children! I love to sing! There lies my musical talent, my voice. Wherever your talent lies, use it to create music with young children. As you adapt musical activities around your gifts and talents, keep these milestones in mind.

Milestones

Twos and Threes

- Love upbeat rhythms and respond naturally through simple movement

- Enjoy playing percussion instruments and experimenting with different sounds

- May become overstimulated by music: need variety and time for relaxation

Threes and Fours

- Can march and play instruments simultaneously

- Begin to understand the concepts of loud/soft, fast/slow, and high/low

- Enjoy using instruments and voices to accompany music

Fours and Fives

- Like to combine chants with movements

- Are able to mimic various rhythmic patterns

- Can keep time to the beat of music by clapping, tapping, and so on

(Gordh, 1996)

Our music program

When I write a lesson plan I select music and activities that are a natural extension of the classroom, integrating the same themes.

When planning for two- to three-year-olds, the length of the lesson is between 15 and 20 minutes with a group size of eight. When planning for three- to four-year-olds, the length of the lesson is between 20 and 25 minutes with a group size no larger than ten. When planning for four- to five-year-olds, the length of the lesson is between 30 and 35 minutes with a group size no larger than 12. Each lesson is presented in a weekly format, sometimes extending the same lesson for several weeks. There are four elements that are always experienced in our music class: we sing, we listen, we play (instruments), and we move. These are the core activities in music and movement development.

We sing . . .

First we sing a song of greetings, without any instrumentation; we use just our voices. We like to sing "Hello Songs" and "Name Game Songs." This centers everybody and gathers us all together, recognizing one another. "Hello everybody, how do you do, how do you do, how do you do. Hello everybody, how do you do. God loves you today." OR "Come on everyone, come on everyone, come on everyone, sing with me. Come on 'child's name,' come on 'Tommy,' come on 'Nicole,' sing with me" (Heyge & Sillick, 1994). While we sing our greeting songs, the children and I tap our knees with our fingers, establishing the beat.

This begins to establish beat competency. Other favorite songs that the children love to sing are call and respond songs as well as simple easy-to-sing songs. Some favorites that you will recognize are, "If You're Happy and You Know It Clap Your Hands," "Aiken Drum," "Old MacDonald," "It's Raining," and "Dinah." Fingerplays are thoroughly enjoyed by young children and can be set to simple familiar tunes. The child has a natural tendency to be active with fingers and hands. The rhythmic quality of a verse, repeated over and over, is reinforced by the movement of the hands and fingers together.

We listen . . .

We play group listening games. "What do you hear?" I will often play a tape with recorded sounds from nature. For example, during a farm theme I will play recorded farmyard animal voices. It is a lot of fun guessing which farmyard animals are "singing." After listening to the tape, ask the children some questions: "Was the animal's voice high or low? Was the animal's voice loud or soft?" Use matching animal illustrations to help integrate sight and sound. "Point to the animal that you just heard."

The weather is another favorite theme to explore in music. "Weather is full of the nicest sounds. Listen very carefully, you can hear the weather 'sing.' What do you hear when you listen to the weather? Does it ping or does it pound? Does it rustle,

strum, or hum?" Children can hear sprinkles and splishes, bangs and whishes. Mumbles and grumbles and rumbles and flashes and crashes! (A. Fisher in Heyge & Sillick, 1994)

There are so many possibilities! Look to nature to get your ideas.

Another listening activity that the children enjoy begins to establish pitch recognition. We call it the "Copy Cat Game." I will ask the children to "tie on their listening ears and copy my voice." "If my voice is high, you need to make your voice high; if my voice is low, you need to make your voice low." I will sing three different intervals of the scale and ask the children to copy what they have just heard, matching their voice to mine. This fun game begins to establish tonality.

We play . . .

Music has a "heartbeat" you can count on. Bang, bang, rat-a-tat-tat! To "know," a child must "touch." So, put an instrument in a child's hand! Percussive instruments are the most appropriate for young children. I use a lot of different kinds of percussive instruments, such as drums, rhythm sticks, shakers, jingle bells, tambourines, sand blocks, triangles, and resonator bars.

Remember the human body can also be an instrument! Suggest that children try drumming on their own bodies. Encourage them to lightly hit their thighs, arms, heads, and tummies. Let them experiment with other ways to make sounds with their bodies (for instance, by snapping their fingers or clapping).

We love to play our instruments along with different kinds of music, feeling the rhythm and establishing a beat. Playing instruments to music allows for much experimentation. I like to expose our children to a wide variety of music. We listen and play along to different styles of music, such as jazz, country western, classical, gospel, and lively multicultural music. Check your local library for lively, diverse music with strong rhythms. Begin to collect music from various cultures. As you play the variety of music, encourage children to play in different ways.

We move . . .

Dance to the rhythm! Many kinds of music make for lots of movement fun. This is a natural mode of being and expression for children. They love to creatively express themselves with their whole bodies. Young children love to crawl and walk, run and jump — they love all kinds of movements just for the sake of being active.

Invite children to act out a song. One of our favorite songs to act out is the old-time favorite, "Teddy Bear Picnic." The children pretend to be teddy bears going into the woods for a picnic. Of course, they need to have a blanket. How can you have a picnic without a picnic blanket? So we use different colored scarves and take them along.

The children march to the woods waving their "blankets" (all to the beat of the music). Once they are in the woods, they spread out their blankets and begin to play around them, trying not to dance on each other's scarves. At the end of the song, we lay down on our blankets because we are all very "tired little teddy bears."

On another occasion, our colored scarves became leaves. I invited the children to each take a scarf. "Pretend it is a leaf floating to the ground, blowing in the wind, etc. Now make the scarves dance to the music." Children are great at improvising.

Songs have moods we can interpret. Play a few songs with very different moods, such as a slow spiritual, a waltz, or an upbeat march. Talk about the mood of the music, and then ask children to move to the music, matching body movement with the tempo of the music. One of the most memorable dance experiences the children and I shared together was creating a "line dance" to the "Boot-Scootin' Boogie" by Brooks and Dunn. I placed a long piece of masking tape (the line) on the carpet in the music room and invited the children to dance on the line. We clapped and stomped, kicked up our heels, and moved to the very lively country western song, all the time staying on the line! What fun we had!

Conclusion

When planning and incorporating music into your early childhood learning environments, start with where you are musically. If you have a basic knowledge of music you'll be okay! Remember, you do not have to be a highly trained professional in music to make music. Allow yourself the time and freedom to be receptive to the children's ability to lead you with their interests, playfulness, and natural love of music. Mix the fun of music with useful specific information. You and your children will find that you have been "tricked into learning new things together."

My resource

I pull from many different resources when planning a music lesson. The most helpful resource (that I heavily rely on) is the MusikGarten curriculum. The resources available through MusikGarten are a tremendous help and very teacher friendly. Planning is made easy and the quality of materials are excellent. (For more information, call MusikGarten, toll free, at (800) 216-6864 — or visit their web site, www.Musikgarten.org.)

References

Gordh, B. (1996). "Music to your ears." *Early Childhood Today, 11*(3) (November/December), A1-A9 (pullout section).

Heyge, L., & Sillick, A. (1994). *Music and movement: The cycle of seasons — Teacher's guidebook and resource materials for group instruction.* Greensboro, NC: Music Matters.

Special thanks for helping to shape this Beginnings Workshop to Kirsti Haugen and Karen Stephens.

Cindy Smtih has been the director of preschool ministries at Holy Trinity Lutheran Church in Littleton, Colorado, for the past 10 years. The preschool has been accredited by NAEYC, under her leadership for seven years. She has a Bachelor of Science degree from Colorado State University, actively serves with the Colorado AEYC and its affiliate group in the Denver Metro area. A mother of three grown boys, Cindy has worked in the field of early childhhood education and child care for 22 years.

Using Beginnings Workshop to Train Teachers by Kay Albrecht

Perky Parent Meetings: Start each parent meeting by teaching parents one or two of the songs that are regularly used in the classroom. Make copies of the words and repeat the song several times until it is well known.

Music Teacher As Resource: Find someone to do special music and movement activities occasionally. Call other schools and see if you can borrow their music teacher once a week or once a month to enrich the music and movement that teachers are already doing.

MUSIC AND MOVEMENT

Music:
The Great Connector

by Thomas Moore

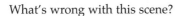

What's wrong with this scene?

"My Girl," one of the teacher's favorite songs, fills the classroom with its upbeat chorus. The four-year-olds jump and dance alongside the teacher. Almost all the children are engaged, except for a few who are happily coloring at a side table. The teacher even pantomimes a microphone and gives each child a chance to sing with The Temptations.

In some ways, nothing is wrong with what I've described. It's wonderful for children to listen to music, either as a main activity or as background sound. But imagine how much more the children would gain if the teacher used music as the starting point for a fuller experience.

What if, once everyone finished dancing, the teacher began to describe when she first heard that song as a girl? What if she brought photos of herself at that age, and some of the clothing styles she wore? What if she talked about the neighborhood and city where she grew up, the foods she ate, the games and activities she and her friends liked?

Then the children are entertained — and much more. They find out who their teacher is as a person. They develop bonds with other children and people in their community. The music is not a disruption to the day but a way to connect different kinds of learning experiences throughout the curriculum.

Music as entertainment for young children is fine. But music used to stimulate growth and development is truly exciting.

Giving children opportunities to connect

I discovered this vital use of music during my childhood. In my neighborhood, music mellowed every part of the day. I heard music at home and church. We sang in the car and on the porch, during family celebrations and before sleep. Not everyone in my family had what people think of as a great voice. We weren't concerned about who had the best voice, or even a good one. We focused on relationships, and singing was part of this. Music connected us to who we were and are.

As a teenager, I drew upon what I learned at home for my first job as a preschool teacher's aide. We used many recordings by children's musician Ella Jenkins. Her songs were, and still are, ideal for young children. They are easy to sing, with very simple rhythms and lyrics. Children enjoy the songs because they can easily join in. They aren't merely watching or listening to an experience; they are part of it, singing together.

In the United States, we tend to present music to children through concerts, as if music is always external. We communicate the message that you have to be especially gifted to play music. Perhaps that's why, by the time children reach elementary school, many say they don't like music, can't sing, or can't dance.

In this strategy, we have overlooked something essential. Children have music in them. Think of how a baby excitedly wiggles his arms and legs when someone sings to him. We were born moving to sound. Children intuitively understand music as a way to connect to themselves and others.

Many traditional children's songs have become popular because they encourage connections. "Patty cake, patty cake" inspires us to play a clapping game together. "London Bridge" fosters interpersonal communication — you can't fall down or "lock 'er up" by yourself. "Farmer in the Dell" helps children understand and focus on relationships. (You might try singing this song early in the school year and see who children "take" as their wife, dog, cat, and mouse, then sing later in the year and observe how relationships have developed and changed.)

The more a child can connect, the more she can make sense of her environment and her emotions. Music can be a catalyst for exploring feelings. You can begin by singing together, "If you're happy and you know it, clap your hands." But don't end there. Ask the children, "What else can we do besides clapping hands and stamping feet to show we're happy?" Talk about what it means to be happy. Bring in photos featuring an array of happy faces. Take photos of your children smiling.

Using music to cultivate connections

1 Use music to redirect children who are misbehaving. If I need to get children's attention, I will sing something I know they like. It can be as simple as a call-and-response version of "Twinkle Twinkle." If I am creating a large group music and movement experience and have introduced one of my songs, such as "Alphabet Boogie," I'll sing it again to redirect children. Switching from talking to singing can quiet a room fast. You'll find your own ways to use music and movement to redirect children.

2 Take advantage of call-and-response songs in other ways. The call-and-response technique makes it possible for children to be immediately involved in making music. Like Ella Jenkins, singer Hap Palmer has recorded many call-and-response songs that you might like to use.

3 Experiment with creative-movement games. Ask children to copy you. Then stop talking and just use actions. Be a butterfly. Swim. Make waves. Play peak-a-boo.

Let a song's lyrics suggest activities. One of my favorites is Ella Jenkins' "This A Way, That A Way." Hands, heads, and hips can all go this-a-way, then that-a-way. Or make two posters, one for each side of a room. Ask children to point to the poster on the right, then the poster on the left, this-a-way and that-a-way.

4 Use the range of your voice. Try peak-a-boo in a very high voice, then in a very low one. Encourage children to find out what their voices can do.

5 When caring for infants, hold them close and hum. It will relax you and build rapport. Have fun whispering or humming in one of the baby's ears, then the other.

6 Find songs that can become games. Let's use my "Paper Bag Boogie" as an example:

We're gonna play with paper bags today.
Let's play with paper bags today.
Now put it on your hand, yes, sir.
What do you have? A glove bag.
Now take it off your hand, yes, sir.
What do you have? A paper bag.
Now put it on your foot . . . a shoe bag.
Now put it on your head . . . a hat bag.
Put some beans in the bag . . . a shaker bag.

The song helps children discover all the places a paper bag can fit — on a hand, foot, or even head. If you plan to use this song, encourage parents to bring paper bags to your center. Children can decorate and write their names on the bags, and talk about where they came from. Now music is part of the experience — as well as art and pre-reading skills.

7 Don't be afraid of repetition. I'll sing "Twinkle Twinkle" a hundred times if children want me to. The children know the lyrics. It has an easy melody. And it was probably first sung to the children by someone close to them. All are components of a rich experience.

8 Use a familiar tune and change the lyrics. Sing about something children are experiencing at your center or elsewhere in their lives. Then encourage children to do the same. This method inspires children to create from knowledge of their environment, a key element of the acclaimed Reggio Emilia philosophy.

9 Use music to explore a variety of cultures and countries. Try a "Meeting New Friends Day." If you pick China, for example, play music from that country. Offer a snack of Chinese food. Talk about or play the games children play in China. If you can, invite a Chinese native to your class to describe his or her homeland.

My friend Robin Felts, a preschool teacher in Charlotte, North Carolina, offers these additional ideas:

10 Pick a tune and dance square-dance style. Children gain social skills by choosing and changing partners.

11 Paint to music. What sort of brush strokes and colors seem to fit with classical music? Jazz? Rap?

Activities and Experiences

When I'm evaluating a musical activity for children, I ask these questions:

■ Are the children singing?

■ Do they sing or play with the lyrics later on, by themselves or with each other?

■ If it's a creative movement activity, are they moving?

■ Do they dance during the activity, or afterwards, on their own?

12 Explore songs written for curriculum themes, from transportation to brushing teeth, colors and shapes to health care.

13 Experience rhythms. Older preschoolers are able to duplicate rhythmic patterns by clapping, stomping, or using rhythm sticks.

Remember, you can move your children towards creativity or away from it. The magic is already in children. You are there to help them discover it. Sing and enjoy!

Thomas Moore, Ph.D., is a keynote speaker, early childhood consultant, children's recording artist, and official musician for the National Head Start Association. He is author of two teacher resource books, *Where is Thumbkin?* and *Do You Know the Muffin Man?* and has produced eight recordings for children. You can reach Dr. Moore at (704) 371-4077 or thomas@drthomasmoore.com with your comments.

Using Beginnings Workshop to Train Teachers by Kay Albrecht

Staff Meeting Extension: Ask each teacher to bring a music or movement activity to the staff meeting and brainstorm ways to extend the activity like Thomas Moore did with "My Girl." Use a curriculum webbing approach to flesh out a variety of ideas.

Songs As Games: Try the paper bag game with teachers. Review the other songs frequently used in the classroom and explore how to make them into games as well.

Expand Recording Library: Ask parents from diverse cultures to share music with you. Create sections in your recording library on all of the cultures represented in your school.

Happy Birthday Music and Movement: Institute a musical gift for children as a part of birthday celebrations. Add a special musical recording to the recording library with the name and birth date of the child written on the recording. As teachers use different recordings, they can remind children that the recording was added to the library on the child's birthday.

Music and Movement Professional Portfolio Entry: Add a list of tried-and-true music and movement activities that you use in your classroom to your professional portfolio. Include a photograph of children participating in one of your best tried-and-true activities. Detail what children are learning as a part of the entry.

Resources for Teachers and Directors

Dowell, R. I. *Mother Ruth's rhymes.*

Dowell, R. I. *Move over Mother Goose.*

Schiller, P., & Moore, T. *Where is Thumpkin?* Beltsville, MD: Gryphon House.

Silsberg, J. *I can't sing book for grownups who can't carry a tune in a paper bag.* Beltsville, MD: Gryphon House.

MUSIC AND MOVEMENT

Learning Through Music:
The Support of Brain Research

by Elizabeth B. Carlton

"Star light, star bright, . . ."
"Ring around the rosey, pockets full of posies . . ."
"The farmer in the dell . . ."

Do you remember singing these simple songs from childhood? If the first part of a familiar song text is given, most of us will finish singing the song, even if we sing it only in thought! As grownups, we may remember the joy experienced while singing and playing musical games with our friends. Often as we hum these melodies, we think of other songs we learned during our early school years, and we realize that we can still sing many of these from memory! I wonder if singing many songs and experiencing other essential benefits music provides will be possible for the majority of our 15 million preschoolers today.

MUSIC! How can children learn or live without it? Music educators have known for years that quality music experiences enhance listening; invite intuitive and steady beat responses; and aid learning of vocabulary, sound and pitch discrimination, emotional responses, creative responses, memory, and many hours of fun for our wee ones. What powerful links to learning might we use within the many aspects of music? It appears that the first three years of a child's life are critical for optimal brain development, for music, and for learning through music. Now brain research is becoming available to support these perceptions. Let's consider some of music's important gifts, supported by research, for the children entrusted into our care.

Music develops listening skills.

Three-year-old Alissa heard her baby sister crying in the infant-care room down the hall. Even though two other babies were also crying, Alissa could recognize the cry of "her" baby! How important keen listening skills are! We have all experienced crying, fussy, or sick children in our care who become calm when quality instrumental music is played. They are listening! If we sing to our three- and four-year-olds, we will probably be asked to sing the song again . . . and again. **Many** listening experiences during the first two years of life are necessary before children actually sing or talk with us. How special the day when we begin to hear their tiny voices joining our voice on repeating or rhyming words in a nursery rhyme, or on the last word and pitch of the song! Songs, instruments, and instrumental music are wonderful ways to develop children's listening skills and awareness of different words and musical pitches.

It is critical that we begin to develop listening skills in our child care settings. Many games about "Listen! What is that sound?" or "Listen! Who is talking/singing?" or "What is making that sound?" encourage children to pay attention to what they are hearing, and even to represent that sound, when we ask, "What sound does the cow (dog, lawn mower) make?"

Moving to music, dancing, playing instruments, and experimenting with materials that make sounds are all helpful to the development of toddlers. "It is the **doing**, in addition to the **listening**, that offers the greatest positive benefit in all aspects of learning, especially in music" (Wilcox, 1999, p. 31). John Feierabend, nationally recognized early childhood music educator, states: "We see a very large difference in the singing capability and musical awareness between children five years old and younger who have been exposed to music and those who have not" (Feierabend, 1999, p. 19).

Listening is necessary to hear same and different letters of our alphabet, words, sounds in our environment, and musical pitches. There will be a lifetime of sounds our children will need to identify. The sooner we encourage listening skills, the more opportunities children will have to develop them.

Music invites intuitive responses.

Children's intuitive responses to high-quality musical recordings is universally positive from birth. Wendy Sims, professor of music education, University of Missouri-Columbia and chair of MENC's Society for Research in Music Education, states, "Researchers have found that, during the preschool and primary years, children demonstrate very positive attitudes toward many kinds of music" (Wilcox, 1999, p. 31). In our child care centers, we may see children moving their whole bodies intuitively to the mood, tempo, and dynamics of music, or to a special instrument they hear in the music long before much language develops. Offer them a scarf or a wide ribbon, and watch their responses grow! Play a Sousa recording, and children will march instinctively! Play a lullaby without words, and notice the intuitive responses! Children will move naturally to almost any musical selection. The seeds of listening encourage intuitive, creative responses to music.

Our challenge as adults is to provide **quality** music for their experiences as we respect the collective needs of children. They also need to be introduced to music they might not have opportunity to hear otherwise. When adults encourage children's intuitive responses to music consistently, children may surprise us as they move creatively to music, and respond with movement representation of the music that makes us want to join in their "dance."

Music is called the universal language because — with no words — all types of music touch children's ears, head, heart, and body, and leave them more alert for having responded.

Music strengthens aural discrimination.

During the first two years of life, young children listen and show us that they recognize many sounds important to them: voices of parents, siblings, and caregivers; sounds in their immediate environment such as their toys, TV, videos, and sounds in the kitchen and in the car. They also recognize musical sounds such as their own name sung, the theme songs for children's TV programs, music an older brother or sister may be practicing, songs sung to them, and the "music" heard in expressive voices of family members and caregivers.

The foundation for responses to aural discrimination is laid from the third trimester *in utero* (Wilcox, 1999, p. 29) and continues through age three. The quality of aural discrimination experiences will affect children's listening, singing, communication, and reading skills throughout their lives. On a nationally televised program, Oprah Winfrey made a plea for parents to sing to their children. Every adult working in child care also needs to take Oprah's request to heart, and sing, sing, sing for the musical needs and aural discrimination skills of their children.

Research shows that infants who are sung to and talked to a lot develop greater phonemic awareness and later develop larger vocabularies. It has been reported that *in utero*, the fetus hears all sounds as "musical" through the amniotic fluid. Toddlers often join in singing with others, and create "infant songs" on their own while they play. Young children who miss these all-important interactions are often less expressive and sometimes delayed in their speech, and may be shy in communicating with others. They may not sing naturally on their own or with a group. This is music's gentle reminder to us that when music tenderly plants the seeds of aural discrimination, it is essential that adult caregivers nurture that seed through *daily musical experiences* that incorporate listening, singing, and moving to music in our child care centers.

Music helps children (and adults!) remember.

When young children sing "Eensy Weensy Spider" or "Clean Up, Clean Up," the underlying steady pulse of the song combined with the active singing pushes the brain to remember the next part of the song, and the next, until we reach the end. This begins as "rote memory" (short term) but does evolve to conscious thought and long-term memory as children mature and songs that have meaning are sung repeatedly by individuals.

A former elementary student of mine recently called to share how much a particular song meant to her in fourth grade. Now that she is teaching fourth grade, she needed a copy of the music (she remembered all of the song!) so her students could sing it with piano accompaniment for their parents. This incident caused me to wonder if we have ever seriously considered the powerful link to learning that lies in all of the aspects of music.

Not only does music strengthen memory, it often wraps feelings or emotions around a song that enhances learning experiences. The Barney version of "I Love You" has placed "This Old Man" on the back of the shelf for two- and three-year-olds! Four-year-olds beam when singing "You Are My Sunshine" or "Hokey Pokey." Think of the pride instilled when singing patriotic songs, the peace experienced singing campfire songs, the religious connections strengthened when singing great hymns of faith. Learning is strongly influenced by emotion — "the stronger the emotion connected with the experience, the stronger the memory of that experience" (Jensen, 1998, p. 73).

For many children today, stress blocks learning avenues. We can relieve much of that stress through daily listening and singing experiences, moving to music, and exploring instrument sounds. We can help create that safe feeling of being a caring "classroom family" through the songs and singing games we lead. Help children develop a "music bank" of aural experiences that provide the foundation for rich memories throughout life.

Music helps children sing tunefully.

Singing experiences with the whole class are the most frequently reported musical activities today. In many classrooms, singing with a recording is the standard way this occurs. In reality, children participate more musically when adults in the classroom lead the singing! Yes! Sing a greeting song! Sing for a birthday! Sing a good-bye song! Often, the tempos recording artists use are faster than young children can imitate. You are right there, and can determine what tempo suits your children. Sing for the joy of singing!

Sometimes, artists forget to sing songs in the children's singing range. If at all possible, please sing **with** your children **in their singing range**, and model the pleasure felt when everyone sings together. The children's natural singing range may feel high or uncomfortable to us at first. Keep in mind that their tiny vocal cords cannot begin to match our adult vocal singing range. We need to "flex" and sing in their range!

Music helps children speak clearly and pay attention.

Become best friends with "neat steady beat." This element of music lies inside all language and music and holds it all together. When children speak nursery rhymes and pat steady beat, they speak more clearly. When teachers encourage children to keep patting steady beat while they sing, no one child races ahead to finish the song first. Children also sing more "in tune," and enunciate more clearly; therefore, singing is more satisfying to everyone. High/Scope Educational Research Foundation's statistics on the steady beat factor suggest that students who demonstrate beat-competence and beat-independence are the same students who perform well in all areas of the academic curriculum (Weikart, 1998).

Music makes transitions in the classroom go smoothly.

All segments of the daily routine — time to work, clean up, go outdoors, have a snack, story time, singing time, etc. — can be connected by using a simple melody such as "Hot Cross Buns" or "Where is Thumbkin?" and creating specific verses for your needs. Before long, children will join you in singing these "new" songs for transition. Many teachers have reported success with this idea. The simplicity and repetition of the melody has given children and adults confidence to sing many other songs.

Singing transitions together provides the time needed for children to finish one activity and be ready for the next. Since young children learn and play totally in the present, their sense of time is not the same as ours. *Their* plan is always the most important plan! Some children need those musical cues and a few extra minutes to finish their project. Try this singing transition to the melody of "Hot Cross Buns":

> Time for a snack! Time for a snack!
> Pass the napkins, pass the juice.
> Time for a snack!

Sing this daily for a week, and then create new words using this same melody for another transition with your teachers next week!

Music helps children cooperate, think, and problem-solve.

Opportunities to cooperate in singing games, action songs, and movement to music are the early childhood active learning precursors to thinking, problem-solving, and memory. Music helps children and adults stay alert. *Music is the essential element for children that touches all ways young children learn.*

Music has received short shrift in today's world of educational values because we cannot measure its immediate importance with hard data. School budgets have cut music programs first. Teachers have allowed others to determine that the gifts of music should be relegated only to nonessential frills and to the area of entertainment. How disappointing. **We have to help others realize that quality music experiences provide** *essential gifts to learning* **found nowhere else.**

Musical instruments provide beginning experiences in pitch, timbre, and texture.

Exploring the various sounds of instruments fascinates young children and, again, can strengthen aural discrimination. They will discover that most instruments make several sounds; they should be encouraged to talk about what they discover.

The music area of the classroom should contain four or five rhythm percussion instruments, a small keyboard, cassette player with headset(s), and several short tapes of songs and instrumental music. Instruments and tapes can be rotated on a monthly basis for maximum learning.

If parents play musical instruments, invite them to share with your class. Older brothers and sisters often need an opportunity to play for others. Here is a perfect opportunity to share music between generations!

Music is FUN! — and fundamental for all young children.

Research suggests that the first three years (**our preschool years!**) are critical for combining music experiences with learning — especially for children in at-risk categories. Because movement almost always accompanies these musical experiences for young children, we should endeavor to provide these double reinforcements in all areas of the curriculum, because **the body, voice, and brain are united for optimal processing.** Grace C. Nash, noted pioneer in American music education, has said for over 20 years that music and movement are the **first languages of childhood** — used before traditional language provides the link to communication. As I have interacted with and observed infants and toddlers for over 40 years, I wholeheartedly concur. Moving and singing are joyful and memorable experiences! Children don't begin to get enough to satisfy their needs.

Daily music experiences in child care can make many valuable connections to our children's language capabilities, memory, physical activity, creative thinking, emotional stability, discipline, and emerging academic success. As brain research begins to support the importance of learning through music, we must continue to find useful ways to make the gifts music provides essential in our daily routine. While music possesses awesome meaning and great value in and of itself, our children will never be able to realize this unless we begin to share these gifts every day. Music's gifts abound around us. Let's use them now to make significant differences in ourselves and with all our children.

References

Feierabend, J. (1999). Quoted in "Make music, America!" *Teaching Music, 7*(3). Reston, VA: Music Educators' National Conference.

Jensen, E. (1998). *Teaching with the brain in mind.* Alexandria, VA: Association for Supervision and Curriculum Development.

Weikart, P. S. (1998). *Steady beat: What we now know.* Ypsilanti, MI: High/Scope Educational Research Foundation.

Wilcox, E. (1999). Straight talk about music and brain research. *Teaching Music, 7*(3), 31. Reston, VA: Music Educators' National Conference.

Elizabeth (Libby) Carlton, Assistant Professor Emeritus of Music, Catawba College, Salisbury, North Carolina, also taught K-6 public school music for 18 years. Formerly the music consultant and author of music publications with Phyllis S. Weikart for High/Scope Educational Research Foundation, she is now the contributing editor for *LifeWay Children's Music Series* of the Southern Baptist Convention. She is serving her 22nd year as church organist, First Baptist Church, Salisbury, North Carolina.

Using Beginnings Workshop to Train Teachers by Kay Albrecht

Music and Movement Self-Assessment: Conduct a self assessment of your music and movement skills. Start by making a list of the music and movement activities you regularly plan and implement in your classroom (play instruments with children, sing songs during transitions, rhythm activities). Then read through the article and add additional music and movement ideas that would expand music and movement opportunities in your classroom. Add the list to your professional improvement plan.

Newsletter Article: Write an article for the school newsletter on the value of music for future academic success to help parents understand how music and movement are wonderful academic readiness activities.

Recording Library: Start a recording library of different kinds of music. Ask each teacher to add a favorite recording to the library. After each teacher does so, take the library to a staff meeting and play some of the selections. Brainstorm with teachers how they might use the recordings in the library.

Music and Movement Scope and Sequence: Observe to see which music and movement activities are done in each classroom in your school. Use the observation as a baseline, and talk with teachers about formalizing the music and movement culture of your school into a sequence chart that can show parents what children are learning from music and movement.

Staff Meeting Performance: Have teachers select a favorite music or movement activity and demonstrate it at a staff meeting. Make sure each teacher has copies of the words of the song and copies of the music for the recording library. Put the ideas together into a staff reference book by combining the songs and putting them in a binder.

Transition Song Talent Search: Have a transition song contest to see who has the best idea for using music and movement for transition activities. Have each contestant perform the transition song with the audience to demonstrate how to use it. Vote for the best presentation and reward the winner with a new CD for her classroom or a gift certificate to order music and movement materials from your favorite school supply catalog.

Music Learning Center: If your school is short on musical instrument and players, put together a rolling music center so that classrooms can share a CD player, a tape recorder, a collection of musical instruments, and the recording library. Keep the center in a central location. Create a sign-up system so everyone gets a turn. As use increases, create a second center with a different variety of instruments and music.

For example:

Infants	Toddlers	Preschoolers	Kindergartners	School-Agers
Sing lullabies.	Play lullabies at nap time.	Experiment with relaxing to various music.	Experiment with using music to signal changes in activities.	Use popular culture music in listening center.
Clean-up song sung by teacher as she cleans up.	Clean-up song sung by teacher as children and teacher clean up.	Clean-up song sung by children.	Experiment with humming clean-up song instead of using words; or playing song on keyboard; or drumming song on drum.	Let children choose various songs to serve as transition songs, i.e., march music to go outside.
Body parts as rhythm instruments (clapping hands, stomping feet).	Introduce cymbals, drums, bells, shakers.	Introduce rhythm sticks, triangles, keyboards.	Introduce instruments like keyboards, flutes, or drums.	Introduce piano, ukulele, violin, flutes, or drums.

MUSIC AND MOVEMENT

Music and Movement Bring Together Children of Differing Abilities

by Carol Stock Kranowitz

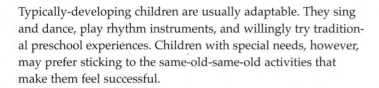

Typically-developing children are usually adaptable. They sing and dance, play rhythm instruments, and willingly try traditional preschool experiences. Children with special needs, however, may prefer sticking to the same-old-same-old activities that make them feel successful.

Whatever the skill level of your preschoolers, a variety of sensorimotor activities in your curriculum can satisfy most children's needs. Music and movement activities, with their flexible structure, can foster every child's creativity and competence.

These stories illustrate how children of differing abilities play together at St. Columba's Nursery School in Washington, DC.

Music and movement allow children to use their imaginations

Quint has spinal muscular atrophy. He has little use of his lower body. As a result of extensive and intensive therapy, however, Quint's upper body is strong. Using a wheelchair, he maneuvers expertly outdoors and inside.

He excels at singing and rhyming, at parachute games, and rhythm band activities. He welcomes enacting playlets, such as "The Gingerbread Man." When the farmers and animals run, run, as fast as they can in pursuit of the Gingerbread Man, Quint joins the chase in his wheelchair. "Watch!" he says. "I can do it myself!"

Quint is decidedly less enthusiastic about up-and-down activity songs, such as "The Noble Duke of York." He mutters, "I hate that song," and who could blame him? Still, the musical activities he shuns are often the ones other children love. While inclusion is the name of the game, and sensitivity to Quint's feelings is crucial, the other children have needs, too. Balancing the needs of all the children is important.

Quint's classmates are a varied bunch. Several children have marvelous motor skills, while others are at various points along the developmental bell curve.

One day the program includes a game designed to strengthen the sensorimotor skills of body awareness, motor coordination, flexion and extension, listening, and beat awareness. We sit in a circle, legs in front.

The singer on the phonograph record instructs us to raise and lower our feet and wave them in big arcs. Most of us do our best, while Quint slumps and scowls.

Next, the singer tells us to move our arms, shoulders, and head — up, down, and all around. Quint can do this. He sits up tall and easily complies with each of these demands.

Then he says, "I have a good idea. Let's lie on our tummies."

Hey! Cool! We have played this game before, but never on our stomachs. Quint's compensatory strategy sounds like fun. We roll onto our stomachs and repeat the activity. Quint cannot raise his toes but can lift his arms, shoulders and head. His agility impresses the other children. "How do you get your arms so high?" one asks.

Pleased, Quint says, "Oh, I'm just really good at that."

Then Giorgio asks, "Can we do it on our backs?"

Following Giorgio's suggestion, we flip over and repeat the game, lifting our body parts into the air. We discover that when our bodies rest on the floor, resisting gravity is easier.

Then Emma wants to try the game lying on our sides. Ooh, that's hard! Charlotte suggests trying it face to face with a partner. That's funny!

Instead of a five-minute warm-up activity, this game absorbs the entire half hour. The children's creative collaboration, regardless of their differing needs, is too purposeful and fun to stop.

Music and movement awaken children's brains

Zack, lost in his own world, exhibits symptoms of autism. His play is comprised of lining up cars and banging together two plastic blocks. His language skills are severely delayed. When he is spoken to, his limited responses are more gestural than verbal.

He seems to enjoy coming to music with his class, but we aren't sure. Sometimes he joins in the movement activities; other times he tunes out.

His classroom teacher remarks, "If only we could learn how to give Zack a jump start!"

One day, I'm rounding up Zack's classmates to come to the music room. The other children are congregating in the corridor. Zack is still in his coat, gazing dreamily at his coat hook, stuck.

I ask, "Are you ready for music, Zack?"

He nods. Otherwise, he doesn't move.

I try a different tactic. I pick him up, give him a bear hug, and rock him from side to side. To the tune of "Twinkle, Twinkle, Little Star," I repeat, "Are you — ready for — music — Zack?"

Suddenly, Zack comes alive. His eyes light up. He laughs. He returns my hug and leans into the rocking motion.

After I set him down, he whips off his coat, hangs it neatly on his hook, and leaps into line. "I'm ready!"

What's happening? Is the combination of singing, deep pressure, and rocking the technique to arouse Zack?

Walking behind him and pressing firmly on his shoulders, I start the song again, making up rhymes that are inexpert, but good enough:

> *Are you — ready for — music — today?*
> *Let's get — moving — here's the — way.*
> *Now we're — walking — down the — hall,*
> *Here we — go — one and — all,*
> *Are you — ready for — music — now?*
> *Let's go — in and — take a — bow.*

Zack loves it and participates in the music class as never before.

Now, to get Zack's attention, we sing while hugging and rocking him. The words needn't make sense, rhyme, or even be there. Humming does the trick, too. The tools that rev him up are melody, deep pressure, and rhythmic motion. This approach helps him get in sync.

Music and movement allow children to be in control.

"No, I won't. You can't make me. I'm the boss of my body," is Fiona's mantra.

Her diagnosis of oppositional defiant disorder (ODD) is not surprising. We know that she struggles to be in control because she feels powerless. To help her learn to be the legitimate "boss of her own body," we require more than a label. What can we offer this contrary, needy child?

Resistive experiences! Resistive experiences benefit everyone. Pressing different body parts against the wall, carrying heavy buckets of sand, kneading mud pies, digging, shoveling, sweeping, and raking are examples of resistive activities. Hard work is fun! And for children who resist everything, resistive experiences can be a potent prescription.

In the music room, a game planned with Fiona in mind employs resistive, stretchy latex bands, often used for exercise or physical rehabilitation. The children sit on the rug surrounding three piles of bands. Red bands are for "kids who feel a little sleepy." Green bands are for kids who feel strong. Blue ones are for kids who feel r-e-a-l-l-y strong. The children consider this information, choose a band, test it, change their mind, select another, and prepare to play.

Fiona, of course, refuses. Children like her cannot be jollied along. The reason is not that they won't participate, but that they can't. That's all right; we are not in a rush here. "I'll leave the extra bands on the rug," I say. "When you're ready, you can choose one."

The game is a follow-the-leader activity. While a lively instrumental rendition of "Yankee Doodle" plays, the first leader steps onto her band, holding the ends in her hands, bending and straightening her knees. The other children follow her example for 16 strong beats.

The second leader centers the band behind her back and pumps her hands forward and back. The others follow. One by one, we go around the circle, and everyone has a turn.

Meanwhile, Fiona sits against the wall, watching attentively. She sees the fun everyone is having — even the teachers. She hears the participants clamor, "Let's do it again!"

Suddenly, Fiona jumps up. "I'll do it," she growls, "but I won't follow any leader!" She snatches a blue band (the most resistive) from the pile.

The music starts again.

Fiona ignores the leaders and invents her own movements. Who could object? At the moment, she is not interfering with anyone, is having a good time, and is gaining physical and motor control of her own body.

Music and movement strengthen children's problem-solving and motor-planning skills

Shep has dyspraxia, which means he has difficulty planning his motions and organizing his body to go through a sequence of unfamiliar movements. Some symptoms of his disorder are poor motor coordination, social immaturity, and emotional insecurity.

The musical game today is tapping rhythm sticks. I splay the sticks out on the rug. "Take one smooth stick and one bumpy stick," I say.

As the other children reach for sticks, Shep hangs back. He wants to participate but doesn't know how to begin.

I hand him a pair, saying, "Here are your sticks. Feel how this one is bumpy; this one is smooth. Now, come be my helper." I open my arms and indicate that he can sit on the floor in front of me.

Shep whispers, "I don't know what to do." I whisper back, "We'll help each other." I adjust the sticks in his hands and place my hands over them. Working as one, we tap his sticks together, on the floor, on his knees, in the air. I guide his motions as the game continues, actually putting the sensation of motion into his muscles. Gradually, I let go. By the end of the game, Shep has scooted back to the circle. He is doing a fairly good job of watching his friends to figure out what to do.

When music time is over, and we have sung the Good-bye Song, and the children are lining up to return to their classroom, Shep turns back and grins. "That was fun," he says. "That was easy!"

Zack, Quint, Fiona, and Shep could very well be placed in classes for children with special needs. However, both they and their typical peers benefit from their inclusion in a mainstream preschool. Here, the emphasis is not on speaking in complete sentences, doing only what the teacher says, or doing things the "right" way. Instead, children are given opportunities to heighten their arousal level, use their imaginations, and develop motor-planning and problem-solving skills.

Thank you, music and movement!

Carol Stock Kranowitz has taught music, movement, and drama at St. Columba's since 1976. She is the author of *The Out-of-Sync Child: Recognizing and Coping with Sensory Integration Dysfunction* (Perigee, 1998) and *101 Activities for Kids in Tight Spaces* (St. Martin's, 1995).

Using Beginnings Workshop to Train Teachers by Kay Albrecht

Observation: Pair teachers up to do observations of each other to discover if any compensation needs to be done for children of differing needs. If areas are identified, brainstorm ideas of how to compensate and try them to see if they work. If they do, remember to put a written record of the compensation idea in the child's file so future teachers can benefit from your discoveries.

Idea Brainstorm: After reading the articles, make a list of all of the ideas that were mentioned. Vow to try one each week until you have tried them all!

Gross Motor Development

Photograph by Subjects & Predicates

GROSS MOTOR DEVELOPMENT

From Cartwheels to Caterpillars: Children's Need to Move Indoors and Out

by Anita Rui Olds

Traditionally, we have relegated children's need for movement to outdoor spaces we call playgrounds. This is unfortunate because children need to move all the time, both indoors and outside, in a multiplicity of ways that neither indoor climbers nor most playground equipment can sufficiently address. Movement and action are essential to children's development in general and to intellectual development in particular. Movement is the gateway to sensing, acting upon, and being affected by the world around us.

Our senses operate by moving, being moved, or being in contact with stimuli that are in motion. We see because our eyes move; forced to stare at a stationary object for long, we cease to see it. We hear because waves of sound strike the eardrum, causing it to vibrate. Taste and smell are also designed to detect changes in stimulation rather than monitor the status quo.

The basic elements of nature — air, fire, earth, and water — are in motion. Whereas the built environment is rigid and immovable, the natural environment is always in flux. And it is nature's rhythmic patterns of change, akin to our own physiological rhythms, which account for the sense of calm we experience in natural settings.

According to Piaget, movement is also essential to the formation of intellect. Piaget called the first stage of intellectual development the sensorimotor stage, when children experience the world primarily through their senses and motoric abilities. He argued that the sensorimotor stage is the bedrock on which the subsequent hierarchy of all intelligence is built. Between birth and five or six years, children's bodies, as much as their minds, are the *organ* of intelligence. Their *bodyminds* require that they move and be moved by their surroundings.

A facet of learning to read may illustrate the relationship between movement and learning. Until children have experiences orienting their bodies in space by going up, on, under, beside, inside, and in front of things, it is possible they

Figure 1: A free-standing climbing structure is only 4 feet by 6 feet by 8 feet high. Its features include: graduated spacing between the rungs for varied challenge; two platforms children can relocate; a slide mounted by a single dowel (left), to be oriented in different directions and removed easily; a swivel hook on a protruding beam (right and center), for suspension of this "bird cage" climber and equipment, such as tire swing, rope, punching bag.

Figure 2: Custom design made maximal use of every cubic inch of the 8 feet by 12 feet available in this infant room. Included are stairs and a slide, a raised "playpen" with view out the window, and places to crawl and explore below. Facing the loft is a waterbed (right) for plopping, resting, and sensory-motor integration. It is backed by mirrors, and surrounded by low, carpeted risers for crawling, sitting, and climbing.

will have difficulty dealing with letter identification and the orientation of symbols on a page. The only difference between a small "b" and a small "d," for example, both of which are composed of a line and a circle, depends on orientation, i.e., which side of the circle is the line on? Zeller found that 98% of the 500 learning disabled children she tested were characterized as being physically *clumsy*. Similarly, Jean Ayres demonstrated that learning disabled children respond more readily to symbolic tutelage after being trained in the use of fundamental motor patterns that promote sensory integration — crawling, falling, rocking, and spinning. Thus, learning disabilities may be caused or exacerbated by immature or improper development of children's sensorimotor systems.

For movement to be developmentally effective, mover-learners must initiate, complete, and receive feedback about the consequences of *their own* movements through space and *their own* operations on materials. Watching something on TV or having an adult move a passive child through an experience will not do. Only by daring, risking, failing, redoing, and succeeding does each child grow. Overprotective caregivers preoccupied with health and safety or the avoidance of legal culpability, who prevent the activity and risk taking essential for normal development, simply retard and prejudice any child's chances for a positive developmental outcome. Especially in working with differently able children, the challenge always should be to identify opportunities for action — find every means possible to maximize the use of capabilities that are strong, and exercise to the fullest extent faculties that are weak. The need for constant exercise is recognized even by contemporary hospital routines where cardiac patients, one day after a heart attack, are urged to get out of bed and slowly walk through their rooms. In sickness as in health, movement is essential to the maintenance of the body's integrity.

Unfortunately, the one thing adults cannot tolerate in children is the incessant, unpredictable movement of their little bodies,

each responding to its own separate drummer. Typically, adults intervene with rules, admonitions, the withdrawal of materials, and the confinement of space in order to *stop* children from moving. In day care, this is most often done by adults controlling access to materials, eliminating gross motor play indoors, and restricting the amount of space available to each group. Thirty-five square feet per child of activity space is usually inadequate for a room to support gross motor play; at least 42 square feet is required. When group rooms are small, instead of restricting each age group to a single cramped space where gross motor play might be intolerable, combining groups and having them share a number of small rooms, one of which might be devoted to gross motor play, is a far more effective strategy.

Conditions constraining children's movement are growing worse in our society, aggravated by severe housing shortages, an influx of people to urban areas, few public playgrounds or vest pocket parks, and long hours spent indoors at day care. Furniture and equipment, coupled with adults' verbal constraints to protect costly material possessions — "Watch out for that . . . " "Be careful of this . . . " "When you turn around make sure you don't . . . " "Lift your hands so that . . . " — put further restraints on children's activity.

Of course, some control is necessary. But to deny activity by relegating it to a playground or a single climbing structure is to halt development at its source. It is doomed to failure. Children's needs to perform and move *must* express themselves despite constraints, prohibitions, and inadequate environmental supports. So children, predictably, fidget in their seats when they cannot get out of them, try incessantly to gain access to prohibited materials behind an adult's back, and continue to chase one another around the room even if it means knocking over furniture and friends. Failure to meet children's varied needs for movement prevents them from having experiences fundamental to their intellectual, social, and physical development.

The first requirement in designing any child care space should be to maximize opportunities for children to move their entire bodies freely and extensively in all directions. Whether indoors or out, our designs must be based on what children *do* when they are moving — the specific ways they use their bodies in relation to space and objects. Children climbing on tables, crawling under chairs, sliding down banisters, balancing on ledges, hiding in closets, and jumping off beds and couches are not simply being obstreperous. Their actions are motivated by a deep, primary, developmental need to explore the multi-faceted parameters of physical activity.

Consider balancing, for example. In addition to walking across a balance beam, there are many ways to vary the balancing experience. You can balance on a beam that is wide or narrow, high or low, sloped or level. You can balance on a rope. You can balance by standing on one foot or two, on your back, on your stomach, seated on your bottom, on your knees, on your hands, on all fours, or on your head alone. You can balance on a stationary object, or on a moving one. In their attempts to experience balancing, children are testing all these possibilities!

Jumping is not only going up and down but discovering the properties of the material jumped in or upon. Will the surface withstand your impact? Will it throw you back, absorb you, tear, rebound, or stretch? Is it different to jump in something hard or soft; into water, sand, hay, or snow? You can also jump *on* something (such as a board), or *over* something (such as a rope or a crack in the sidewalk), or to *different heights*, or *across* things (a puddle or a creek) that may be stationary or in motion. You can jump on flat surfaces or inclines. You can jump *through* things (like hoops). You can even jump in a seated position (on a balloon or inner tube) and bounce. All these are variations of the one simple experience, jumping.

Similar observations can be made about rolling, throwing objects, crawling, and hanging that barely touch the surface of the range of movements children employ when they are being difficult, active creatures underfoot. Play equipment not only needs to be safe, indestructible, maintenance free, operable without adult supervision, and cheap — it also needs to be based on the range of movements children engage in spontaneously, and on a refined set of developmentally sound assumptions.

Three things seem essential:

- Extensive experiences in the natural world and the inclusion of natural elements indoors;

- Identifiable places for gross motor play inside; and

- Use of lofts and varied types of equipment to encourage children's use of their bodies continuously.

Because of nature's profound effect on our physiology, children deserve and require extensive experience in the natural world. Nature is the teacher and the healer. More important than an outdoor play structure are experiences with sand, water, hills, trees, rocks, bushes, worms, butterflies, birds, and sunshine. Amidst these, children will get all the motor experiences they require. The original playscapes were the fields and woods, paths, and streams outside children's homes. Urban child care centers must strive to provide experiences in nature first and foremost.

Indoors, areas for active play should be available to children continuously, unless they are free to move outdoors at will. Scheduled access to a multi-purpose room is insufficient if this happens only once a day. The active area is best located within each group room, near the major pathways, and not in a corner. Equipment to support climbing, crawling, hanging, swinging, and sliding is most desirable.

The climber for three to five year olds illustrated in Figure 1 is only 4 feet by 6 feet. It does, however,

Figure 3: Portable and inflatable equipment, such as this motor-operated air mattress, provide motoric challenges for children of different ages.

Figure 4: Only two can share in quiet play on this small crow's nest 5 feet above the floor. The access ladder, requiring conscious placement of hands and feet, "tells" children how high they are, and provides a way to practice climbing.

require additional space around it for access and the slide. In Figure 2, the available activity space in a room for eight infants was only 8 feet by 12 feet. However, custom design took advantage of every cubic inch to provide babies opportunities to crawl or climb steps, slide, hide in a semi-enclosure, be placed up high to see out the window and make eye contact with adults, and rest or wiggle on a waterbed. Placing hooks in ceilings (even if suspended) or installing a beam across the narrow portion of a room can enable suspension of swings, jolly jumpers, net chairs, punching bags, trapezes, ropes to shimmy up, etc. Portable equipment such as air mattresses (Figure 3), tunnels of fun, mini-trampolines, hammocks, foam- and air-filled wedges, bolsters, mats for tumbling, balance beams, rocky boats, etc. can be shared among groups provided there is space in each room to use them. In some situations, a freestanding structure — slide, climber, or playhouse — either permanent or collapsible, is appropriate. Suspension bridges, which are easy and inexpensive to build, provide genuine motoric challenge for body control.

In addition to specific equipment for gross motor play, any opportunity to climb upon, under, or through a structure enables children to exercise their large muscles, even while playing quietly. Changes in level should be intentionally introduced for their educational and therapeutic value. Their design possibilities are infinite. For example, in Figure 4, climbing is required to reach a small crow's nest where two can engage in quiet play. Young children enjoy perching up high as much as they enjoy working on the floor. Their cognitive maps of rooms are shaped by experiences that allow them to kinesthetically experience and look at spaces from different perspectives. Floors and horizontal surfaces can be lowered or raised; hard or soft; textured or smooth; solid or slatted; flat, inclined, or wavy; made of natural or man-made materials. These include water mattresses and air mattresses, sacks of beanbag pellets, trampoline, nets, suspension bridges, and other resilient materials.

Carpeted risers can serve as objects to climb and crawl over, as supports for toddling, and as play and sitting surfaces for adults and children alike. Whenever a platform is higher than 2 feet, the surface underneath can be designed with varying degrees of enclosure as a crawling and hiding place. The ceiling of the space below can be decorated with mirrors, mylar paper, mobiles, graphics, and textures. If the platform is built into a corner or is L-shaped, several distinct zones, both above and below, can expand the range of movement experiences and the available square footage of a room.

Few creatures alive are busier or more energetic than the preschool-age child. When something moves, it is alive. When it moves easily, in accordance with its own structure, it is healthy and functioning well. Healthy, well-functioning children are free to locate themselves in space, assume different body postures, create their own boundaries, have access to different territories, manifest power, and fulfill their potential. The ideal child care environment provides unending opportunities for children to learn to move and to learn by moving because it conceives of all surfaces, and the entire ambiance, as an invitation to use their bodies and their senses in meaningful and challenging ways.

*Portions of this article appeared in **Human Ecology Forum**, Winter 1980. All environments designed by Anita Olds and Associates. All photographs taken by Anita Rui Olds.*

Anita Rui Olds, Ph.D., a developmental and environmental psychologist, pioneered the innovative design of environmental facilities for children in hospitals, day care centers, schools, therapeutic and special needs settings, museums, outdoor recreational areas, and medical and holistic health offices throughout the United States and Canada. Principal of her own design and consulting firm, Anita Olds and Associates (Woodacre, California), and lecturer in the Eliot-Pearson Department of Child Study, Tufts University, she consulted widely to architectural and design firms and child care programs, and conducted workshops giving users skills to improve the quality of the places in which they heal, work, and grow. Anita was the author of *Child Health Care Facilities: Design Guidelines and Literature Outline* and co-author of *The Architectural Prototype Document: Study for the Development of Day Care Centers in State Facilities.*

GROSS MOTOR DEVELOPMENT

Kids Gotta Move:
Adapting Movement Experiences for Children with Differing Abilities

by Carol Stock Kranowitz

Birds gotta sing, fish gotta swim, and kids gotta MOVE AND TOUCH. Moving and touching are how children first learn about the world. Feeling the sun and grass on their skin, throwing and catching balls, stretching their arms to the ceiling, climbing jungle gyms, and running in great circles are examples of ways that children gain the important information they require to function well. Nature's plan is for young children to absorb sensory knowledge through their skin, muscles, and joints as a foundation for more complex learning.

Typical children move and touch easily. Children with differing abilities, however, often avoid gross motor experiences, although they need them most.

Various reasons may cause this avoidance. Conditions like cerebral palsy or spina bifida may prevent them from moving easily. Subtle problems with motor coordination may make them clumsy. A poor sense of balance may make them feel tipsy. An inability to interpret sounds, sights, touch sensations, or other people's rapid motions may cause them to withdraw from movement experiences.

How can we help children with differences join in the fun and gain the movement experiences they need?

■ We can *observe* them to discover their strengths and learning styles.

■ Because teachers see children differently, we can **brainstorm** to uncover what activities they crave or avoid in various situations. For instance, some children will prefer outdoor to indoor activities, or small group to large group activities. Some will try new experiences only with a favorite teacher nearby. Some will move better in the morning, when they are fresh, or in the afternoon, after warming up.

■ We can *adapt* movement experiences to meet their individual needs.

■ We can be *flexible* — especially when they are not.

Let's look at examples of children, their difficulties, and the adaptations that teachers have found for atypical children at St. Columba's Nursery School in Washington, DC. These adaptations are generalizable to other children in many situations.

Child/Difficulty: Ned has spina bifida. Paralyzed below the waist, he requires canes and heavy leg braces to walk.

Adaptations: Ned's inner drive to move is intense. To let him enjoy swinging without the danger of falling, the school has purchased a safety bucket swing seat. To let him experience sledding, a teacher sits on a plastic saucer, puts him on her lap, and slides with him down the snowy hill.

When his group enacts "The Three Billy Goats Gruff," Ned wants to be the Big Goat, but cannot climb the aluminum ladder to trip-trop across the bridge. A teacher with a strong backs lifts him to the bridge, and he pulls himself across in a sitting position, making booming sounds with his braces.

His pleasure in participating in motor activities is so great that other children want to swing, sled, and trip-trop "just like Ned." Thus, the adaptations that the teachers make are not only therapeutic, but also instrumental in helping him socialize with his peers.

Child/Difficulty: Leticia, legally blind, is reluctant to move.

Adaptation: Discovering that she can discern bright, shiny objects, teachers stick strips of metallic duct tape at eye level on the walls and floor. Soon Leticia is able to find her way to the classroom, bathroom, and playground. Her growing independence in getting from place to place makes her feel more adventurous. The more she moves, the more she can move.

Child/Difficulty: Jody has difficulty coordinating both sides of his body. Teaming his hands, arms, legs, or eyes to work together is hard. He avoids movement activities requiring bilateral coordination, like riding tricycles, keeping a beat with rhythm sticks, and catching and throwing balls.

Adaptation: The teachers replace the standard playground ball with a huge, colorful beach ball that is easier for Jody to watch and catch. He tastes success and begins to participate in other movement activities.

Child/Difficulty: Manuel has emotional problems. He responds to the presence of other children by crouching in a corner and shouting, "Go away!" Only when he feels unthreatened can he run, jump, balance, swing, and climb.

Photograph by Nancy P. Alexander

Adaptation: The teachers devise a plan to offer him the movement experiences he craves. They take turns spending a few moments alone with him after his classmates have left the playground. He welcomes the chance to move freely, without being distracted by other children. When he comes indoors, he is calmer and more able to interact.

Child/Difficulty: Connor has tactile defensiveness. Because touching or being touched frightens him, he reacts to ordinary touch sensations with flight-or-fight responses. Connor avoids playground equipment like swings, trikes, seesaws, and monkey bars because he cannot tolerate handling them.

Adaptations: The teachers notice that although Connor avoids touching objects with his hands, he enjoys movement experiences like running, balancing, kicking, and jumping. Thus, they inaugurate the "Mini-Olympics" with events designed to engage him. One teacher chalks a racetrack on the blacktop so Connor can run in his individual lane without the threat of bumping into other athletes. Another teacher supervises the seesaw and invites the children, one by one, to walk across. Another teacher hauls out a trampoline and stands guard while each child jumps. The Mini-Olympics include broad jumps and ball kicking events as well. Connor gets a workout!

Child/Difficulty: Bo has vestibular/proprioceptive dysfunction, a neurological problem affecting his ability to process sensations from gravity, movement, and his own muscles and joints. Unable to maintain his balance, Bo falls frequently and has trouble regaining an upright position. Bo also has trouble with motor planning, the ability to plan and execute a movement in a smooth sequence. Although he can crawl into the big concrete pipe in the sandbox, getting out is difficult. Because moving is difficult and scary, he spends most of his time lying down, lost in his own world.

Adaptations: At circle time, the teacher provides everybody with a one-legged T-stool. (To make a T-stool, take two pieces of 2" x 4" wood, each piece about 12" in length, and screw them together into a "T" shape.) Sitting on an unstable T-stool requires balancing, no easy task for Bo; but when he masters it, his posture and attentiveness immediately improve.

To provide Bo with motor planning experiences, the school invests in a large barrel made of thick foam. Holding the barrel upright, a teacher instructs Bo, step by step, how to climb onto a chair, grab the lip of the barrel, lift one leg, and slide in. Bo is delighted with his success! The teacher gently tips the barrel onto its side, and, after many repetitions, Bo learns how to crawl out, all by himself. •

Child/Difficulty: Andrea's fine and gross motor skills are excellent. She moves gracefully, plays beautifully with others, and is particularly creative with playdough, markers, and small manipulative toys. However, she avoids activities like jumping into leaf piles, digging in the sandbox, and sloshing through puddles. "No," she says tearfully, "I can't do that."

What is her problem?

Her babysitter! Her babysitter insists that Andrea stay clean, warning her every morning to "play like a young lady and stay away from dirt."

Adaptations: The teachers find ways for Andrea to enjoy activities that will satisfy her yearning to move without making her fearful of her caregiver's disapproval. They staple crepe paper streamers to long cardboard tubes so that Andrea may run with the wind. They provide her with hoops to roll across the blacktop. They assure her that swinging, sliding, jumping on the trampoline, and pedaling tricycles will not soil her clothes. Indoors, Andrea dances with silk scarves, moves through obstacle courses, and plays "Ring Around the Rosy." The teachers help Andrea balance her two worlds so that she can participate in the gross motor activities she loves without causing her emotional stress.

Child/Difficulty: Joe has an auditory processing problem. Following directions, listening to stories, asking and answering questions, and communicating with his peers are difficult. Joe is a silent, inflexible child who seeks to control people and objects.

Joe's strengths are his gross motor and visual skills. He likes working puzzles, building with blocks, and rearranging equipment, indoors and out. However, he cannot verbally express his ideas or needs and becomes easily frustrated when things don't go his way.

Adaptations: The teachers give Joe opportunities to express himself through movement. One teacher organizes a "Follow the Leader" game. When Joe's turn comes, he leads the children creatively and successfully, up, down, through, and around the playground equipment.

Another teacher invites him to help her plan an obstacle course, saying, "Show me how you'd plan it." Joe arranges the canvas tunnel, balance beam, foam barrel, gym mats, wooden ramps, and A-frame ladders. He tests his design, makes adjustments, and nods with satisfaction. The obstacle course is completely different from the teacher's plan. She says, "Wonderful!"

Joe hears her — and beams. Kids gotta move and touch. Let's observe, brainstorm, make adaptations, and be flexible so that active play works for every child!

Carol Stock Kranowitz has taught music, movement, and drama at St. Columba's since 1976. She is the author of *The Out-of-Sync Child: Recognizing and Coping with Sensory Integration Dysfunction* (Perigee, 1998) and *101 Activities for Kids in Tight Spaces* (St. Martin's, 1995).

GROSS MOTOR DEVELOPMENT

Roughhousing as a *Style* of Play

by Rick Porter

Roughhousing is what children do naturally with each other. Chasing each other, pushing, shoving, tickling, tackling, tripping, wrestling, wrangling, jostling, grabbing, and doing what studies show all species of young mammal siblings do. Anyone who has raised kittens or puppies or a home full of young children can tell you about roughhousing. Typically, a father, uncle, older siblings, or mother starts this by wrestling on the bed or out in the back yard with a child. Roughhousing is a familial style of play. It starts in the family.

For the past 20 years, I have studied and worked with this style of play to help make it more available to children in child care, preschool, and camp programs. By establishing guidelines for teachers and children, it can be a safe and fun activity for all involved. Roughhousing is always voluntary for the children who want to participate. Planning, understanding, and appropriate limit setting makes it a positive experience.

The key to its success is to start simple and encourage the children to have fun. "London Bridge Is Falling Down" is the age old roughhousing game. Mats or soft grassy areas to fall on are essential. Freeze tag, controlled snowball games, balloon stomps, sock bops, and pillow fights are other traditional roughhousing activities. Wrestling games, tag teams, and pushing games are ways in which children can play with each other in a safe, fun, and physical way. Teacher and child comfort levels as well as children picking their own partners are important considerations to make these rough and tumble activities successful. I have designed some equipment that we call **Boppers** and **Pushers**. These are soft, foam filled items that children can use in roughhousing play with each other.

I thought it would be interesting to ask teachers who have roughhoused with children for many years to share what they saw as some of the long-term benefits to their programs:

"Quiet children gain self-confidence by being able to participate. It is a good ice breaker — so good that we give our parents an opportunity to do it with their children on Parents' Night. It gives them a special awareness and a sense of their bodies in space. The balls, the boppers, and wrestling are activities during our program's gross motor time. On rainy days and when the yard is icy, the rough-housing helps the children have active play in our multipurpose room."
— *Sharon Richter, teacher, Union Church Christ Family Weekday Program, Hinsdale, Illinois*

"It is non-competitive, but children who want competitive interactions get benefits as

well. It builds body self-esteem. It also cuts down on the pushing and shoving during regular activities. With the hard winter this year, we were indoors much more. Roughhousing gave us more indoor gross motor options for activities. It helps older children become more aware of their strength and to help them control their bodies and in setting good limits."
— *Irene Denty, director, Lexington Afterschool Program, Lexington, Massachusetts*

"The children I have worked with over the years have really encouraged me to continue to make this available to them. One 11-year-old expert says, "It's a good way to get your energy out without hurting anyone and it is lots of fun. My mom likes to get me with the boppers sometimes."
— *Adam Neugebauer, Redmond, Washington*

In a time when childhood seems to be compressed into megabytes and we rush children to be computer literate, it is important to listen and respond to what children like and want as a part of their play day. Roughhousing is a natural expression of children's exuberance, joy, and affection for each other. We owe it to their childhoods to find as many outlets for their active play and physical expressions between each other as possible.

Roughhousing Guidelines

1. Define and clear a specific area for the activity. Use mats and pillows to soften an indoor area. Use grass or mats outdoors

2. Adults should supervise.

3. Remind children that this is meant to be a FUN activity.

4. Participation is voluntary and children should pick their own partner.

5. No hitting, kicking, biting, hair pulling, or choking.

6. Take off shoes, belts, earrings, and other impinging articles.

7. Respect one's face, eyes, and genitals as sensitive areas.

8. Allow a minimum of half an hour for the activity.

Rick Porter is the owner and manager, along with his wife, Suzanne Dame Porter, of the Rainbow River/Rainbow Rising Child Care Centers in Southern California. Rick is a graduate of Pacific Oaks College and has been teaching the Positive Roughhousing program for over 15 years. He has produced a video, "Roughhousing: A Guide to Safe Fun Physical Play."

GROSS MOTOR DEVELOPMENT

Moving Teachers to Move Children

by Margie Carter

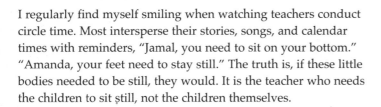

I regularly find myself smiling when watching teachers conduct circle time. Most intersperse their stories, songs, and calendar times with reminders, "Jamal, you need to sit on your bottom." "Amanda, your feet need to stay still." The truth is, if these little bodies needed to be still, they would. It is the teacher who needs the children to sit still, not the children themselves.

Children always bring their bodies to our classrooms (or should I say their bodies bring them?). Yet very quickly they get the message that it is only their minds we value. Indoors, where children spend most of their time, those bodies are merely tolerated, if not punished. True, teachers dutifully schedule gross motor time on curriculum plans. But the typical goal for this is to have children run off excess energy so they will be more manageable during the teaching activities taking place inside. Those who understand the importance of physical development in young children's lives still tend to plan for it as an activity separate from other learning.

The articles in this issue of **Beginnings** remind us that motion is central to the needs of young children, not only in developing their bodies, but their minds, memories, emotions, and communication systems. Teachers may have covered this information in their child development classes, but most often they haven't uncovered the implications of it for their teaching. What will enable teachers to understand and plan for an integrated development of the minds and bodies in their care? Self-awareness, careful observation, and experimentation are in order, laced with a disposition of curiosity and a willingness to risk a little. The following training ideas can be done during a portion of each staff meeting or they can become a series of workshops or a full day's training on movement for learning.

Survey yourself

Soon after we leave adolescence, the primary involvement in sports for most adults is as a spectator. Even with our country's current interest in health and fitness, adults are encouraged towards sedentary activities — sitting for reading, writing, watching sports and entertainment on TV. Power tools now take the effort out of any domestic chores, and we are encouraged to let our fingers do the shopping, visiting, learning, and communicating via telephone or computer.

Most of us need practice in becoming reacquainted with our bodies. As we age, we get into habits that are not especially healthy — physically, mentally, or emotionally. We get tired, lose stamina and endurance. Some of us ignore our aches and pains, while others are defeated by them. When anxious or bored, many of us tend to mentally or emotionally check out of our bodies. No wonder the incessant movement of children tends to drive us nuts. We can hardly remember what it's like to be fully alive and learning in our bodies. This is an occupational hazard for teachers and a detriment to our intentions for children's learning.

Strategy: Childhood memories

When teachers can recapture a memory of exhilaration and power in their bodies, they can better appreciate and provide for it with children. Whether in a staff meeting or class, ask teachers to close their eyes and make themselves comfortable. Tell them to think back to their childhoods and find a favorite time when they were physically active. What was the setting? Who was there? How did they get into the activity? What did it feel like while they were doing it? How did it feel afterward? Did they get any encouraging or discouraging messages about this from others? Is there a reason they stopped doing this activity as they grew older, or is it still something they do?

In a group discussion about these memories, teachers often reveal the excitement of pushing their (or someone else's) limits.

They have shared experiences of climbing the tallest tree; jumping or swinging higher than was allowed; challenging the wind, waves, or wrestling opponents with their bodies. A discussion of these experiences reminds teachers why children do what they do, and perhaps alerts them to unconscious feelings of their own loss in this area. Childhood memories can lead to insights regarding teachers' own comfort levels with physically challenging action and safety factors. The discussion can spark new considerations on how to safely plan for children to take physical risks.

Strategy:
What's your move?

When teachers develop self-awareness about the ways they themselves process sensory information, they are better able to recognize and plan for this in children. Ask teachers to consider which of the following things they do to help them calm, organize, and alert themselves as they go about their lives. This can be done through a guided visualization or by asking a series of questions.

■ When you have a difficult task which requires sitting and concentrating, what little activities do you do to get yourself started and to keep yourself going (i.e., doing your taxes, writing a report, analyzing a problem)?

■ When you are all wound up and need to calm down and focus, what motions do you take yourself through (i.e., after an emotional exchange, reading or watching a mystery or action-packed story, participating in some competitive activity)?

■ When you are tired and having trouble paying attention, what strategies have you developed to keep yourself alert (i.e., driving late at night, sitting in church, listening to a lecture)?

Discoveries from these discussions help teachers recognize some basic sensory integration principles. Responses can be listed in columns on chart paper according to the type of activity they represent.

Sometimes they are oral activities — sucking (on candy, a bottle, or a finger) tends to be calming, while chewing (on candy, gum, a bagel, or pen) is organizing, and crunching (on pretzels, carrots, or a pencil) is alerting.

Tactile activities may include clenching teeth, pushing hands together, popping fingers, biting pencils, applying lotion, scratching, stretching, changing positions frequently, and changing the temperature.

Visual, auditory, and *kinesthetic* activities might be changing the lighting; using a highlighting pen; making a chart; color coding items; listening to music, the radio, or background noise; humming, tapping, rocking, or jiggling parts of the body.

Teachers can end this activity by brainstorming ways to help children meet these needs — things to chew on, stickers to lick, different textured pillows or mats to sit on, playdough with different additives, wet sponges to throw against the fence, different colors and lighting in different areas of the room, a supply of Walkmen®, singing or chanting their conversations or answers to questions, places to hang by the arms, heavy things to carry from place to place, vacuuming, sweeping, mopping up, digging, raking, hoeing.

Survey your children

When teachers tell kids to sit still so they can pay attention, it usually really means the teachers need help in paying attention. They need help in recognizing the sequence of physical development in young children and the implications of their bodies in particular motions. This awareness will allow teachers to plan for individual learning needs and refine their general child development knowledge.

Strategy:
Observe and tell

I like to give teachers specific observation assignments so that they will recognize the intention and purpose that is embedded in children's movements. Ask teachers to identify two of the most active children and the most inactive and to make them the focus of a series of observations. Recording specifically what they see children doing when they are moving, specific ways they use their bodies in space and in relation to objects and materials, gives teachers ample evidence for discussion with their coworkers.

After teachers have the chance to share their observations in pairs or small groups, record examples of actions on a chart listing the types of movements that make up the development of physical and motor skills in early childhood.

■ Gross motor activity — movement of the entire body or large parts of it

■ Fine motor activity — using the small muscles of the body and its extremities

■ Perceptual motor activity — the mind and body working together with spatial, temporal, and sensory awareness

■ Sensory integration — the nervous system processing information to and from the brain

Survey your environment

If they are intentionally considering physical development, most teachers think of the outdoors or designated large motor room in their planning. Their classrooms are most likely set up to reduce large motor activity — running, climbing, and jumping. Because children need to move to learn, I want teachers to consider how to *encourage* movement through the arrangement they set up in the learning environment.

Strategy: Take another look

Ask teachers to map out their room mentally or on a piece of paper. Then begin to assess each area, considering where there are provisions for visual, auditory, tactile, and kinesthetic learning. What about the arrangement and materials will help the children know and be comfortable with where their bodies are in relation to their environment? Are there places to climb and crawl in order to explore spatial relations *while* they are engaged in cognitive or social functions? What physical experiences in the room help them develop body control to work against gravity, to learn what is right side up, upside down, left, right, horizontal, and vertical?

It's likely that teachers have never considered these things in planning their environments and procuring materials. Charts posted on the wall for noting ideas that occur to them in the weeks following this discussion will help teachers continue to think about these physical needs of children as they move about the room.

Survey your curriculum plans

In her article, Anita Olds reminds us that in Piaget's theory of development "the sensorimotor stage is the bedrock on which the subsequent hierarchy of intellectual development is built." Teachers are probably thinking about hands-on activities, but are they planning for *body-on learning*? General training strategies which have participants moving about the room or physically taking a stand or using their bodies to represent their thinking will give them a taste of what this is like.

Here are a few specific ways to give teachers a new learning experience to reflect on and some tools for evaluating their curriculum plans.

Strategy: Sensorimotor exploration

To help teachers understand how "the origins and development of intelligence itself seem to be intimately linked to basic movement patterns in our behavior," provide them with new materials to explore or a task to learn without talking. In the January 1993 **Beginnings Workshop**, I described two training strategies which can be adapted for this purpose.

Give small groups of teachers a large supply of simple open-ended materials to play with uninterrupted for an extended period of time. Tell them to nonverbally explore the materials as if they have never seen them before — arranging, manipulating, and transforming the materials in any way that helps them get to know them. After a period of time has passed, suggest they use the materials as props in dramatic play, assuming roles and talking with each other if they'd like. Finally, tell the teachers to use the materials to create a game with rules that they create as they go along.

In the debriefing discussion, teachers have an immediate experience from which to create a list of what they learned about the materials, themselves, and their playmates through this sensory exploration and movement. In addition, they have the opportunity to consider some new materials and revised rules for moving about the room for learning.

Strategy: Ages and stages for adults

Ask teachers to stand up and, without talking, arrange themselves in a line from the youngest to the oldest. Give no further instructions, but observe all the strategies they use as input into the debriefing which follows. The experience of having to sort themselves out and invent ways of understanding and communicating conveys new insights into the role of movement in children's acquisition of knowledge and communication skills.

Strategy: Make a list and check it twice

As a group, have teachers brainstorm a list of physical actions they typically see children engage in — running, jumping, balancing, throwing, rolling, crawling, hanging, and so on. Then have them use this list to review their most recent curriculum plans. How could any of these learning goals, materials, or themes be explored through the physical activities on our checklist? Make a list, try some of the ideas out on the spot, evaluate, and review the list again. Encourage teachers to make this a habit in their planning and in reviewing how things went.

Survey your bias

Teachers do well to recognize that the value they place on motor activity is directly related to the time allotted and the messages, direct and indirect, they give children regarding the use of their bodies. Are teacher communications during outdoor or other large motor time focused only on safety and taking turns? Does the teacher's current relationship with his/her body or any female social conditioning impact the emphasis given on involvement with physical activity? Are there any differences in the kind of attention and recognition that boys and girls receive? Are the needs for movement and independence of differently abled children planned for or ignored? Is there only one way for children to "show me you are listening" or are they encouraged to find and show their own way of listening, one which really works for their needs?

It's worth ending any training session with the acknowledgment that the work of a teacher requires that we be in our bodies in ways that are not entirely normal — having eyes in the back of our heads; sitting in chairs not made for our size; continually lifting, bending, squatting, and avoiding mental evacuations when things get too stressful. Perhaps the most valuable text-book for teachers has yet to be written — *Zen and the Art of Caring for Children*. To keep our own mind and body integrated, we need the art of mindfulness, attentive breathing, and deep belly laughing, not to mention salaries that would afford us membership in health and fitness clubs.

Somewhere I heard and then repeatedly learned in my own life that new behavior is made possible through physical change.

This adage brings children and teachers great hope for our learning, if only we keep on moving.

Recommended resources

Gilroy, P. J. *Discovery in Motion: Movement Exploration for Problem Solving and Self-Concept.*

Gilroy, P. J. *Kids in Action: Developing Body Awareness in Young Children.*

Gilroy, P. J. *Kids in Motion: An Early Childhood Movement Education Program.*

Trott, M. C., with M. K. Laurel & S. L. Windeck. *SenseAbilities: Understanding Sensory Integration.*

Above resources available from:

Therapy Skill Builders
3830 East Bellevue
PO Box 42050-Y
Tucson, AZ 85733
(602) 323-7500

Margie Carter teaches community college classes and travels widely to consult and speak. She is the producer of numerous staff development videos and co-author of six early childhood books, including *Training Teachers: A Harvest of Theory and Practice*, *The Art of Awareness, Side by Side: Mentoring Teachers for Reflective Practice*, and *Designs for Living and Learning*. Margie believes that teachers should be educated in ways that parallel what we want them to do with children. Active in the Worthy Wage Campaign, Margie is stubbornly passionate about issues of peace and justice.

Creative Dramatics

CREATIVE DRAMATICS

Drama:
A Rehearsal for Life!

by Julia Gabriel

I remember an 11-year-old child in England starting speech and drama classes to learn skills of acting, characterisation, voice projection, poetry reading, and storytelling. She was a quiet, timid introvert. The classes were a great success — within one short year this shy violet was comfortable taking on the role of a character, breathing life into scripted words. The parts she played enabled her to sparkle, safe behind the mask of another person. This child was me! Speech and drama classes gave me the ground to blossom into a performer, happy to open up as long as I was playing a role. I progressed through a series of exams, gaining awards and medals for speaking verse and prose, acting, and eventually at age 18, using my own voice for public speaking. Years later as a mother, I returned to dramatic arts, studied to teach, and set up my own studio at home.

Drama as an ideal learning medium

Creative dramatics aims, traditionally, to develop the performer. More important for me was the discovery that the by-products of learning performance skills are major life skills:

- confidence
- communication skills
- command of language
- development of imagination
- physical freedom
- responsibility
- sensitivity to others
- concentration

Today there are over 10,000 students in our programmes at any one time, acquiring these skills through the exciting medium of drama. Our classes are based on the belief that drama provides all the ingredients for an ideal early learning situation:

- Stimulation — drama allows for stimulation of all the senses

- Motivation — small groups of 8 to 12 children of a similar age who appreciate each other, led by a teacher who enjoys making discoveries with them and celebrates their successes, provides tremendous motivation to participate

- An environment free from pressure — a drama room is a secure space (no watchers or it becomes theatre and can be threatening) that allows students to take risks

- A good model — a teacher who provides good expressive communication skills, listens, and sees the world through the child's eyes

Why is drama successful?

Drama students are valued as important members of a group. They look forward to their weekly classes, the highlight of the week for many, because they love taking part in dramatic projects and adventures. It is important to draw the distinction between performance and drama. In a drama class there is o pressure to perform, only encouragement to participate and learn by taking part. As confidence grows a student may want to perform. This is desirable but should remain optional. "Readiness to perform" is tied to confidence and must be allowed to simmer gently until ready.

The beauty of drama for the shy child is the ability to get lost in the crowd. Slowly, confidence emerges. The timid become braver and learn how to offer and accept ideas from the group. When a child feels comfortable taking he'll start taking responsibility for his ideas. The emerging personality develops through oral language, the tool we use to make friends and take part in a class. By playing a role in the security of a drama class, we rehearse for life.

Stepping into life through drama

Drama is an extension of play, involving ritual and structure. As adults we use it all the time. If we want to get faulty merchandise exchanged we play the role of He Who is in Need of Help:

Excuse me. I do hope you can help me. There seems to be a problem with this machine. . . .

As Mum at pack-away time, chameleon-like we change into She Who Must Be Obeyed:
Right! I want to see all these toys in the basket in one minute!

We slip easily from one language register to another, subconsciously suiting the words and accompanying gesture, or paralanguage, to the situation. Children are even more sensitive to language than we are. They enter into the drama of similar situations readily and easily through imagination — exercising language previously heard but unused — and communication skills modeled on previous experience.

The teacher's role

Child drama is easy to enter, through the imagination. All the teacher or parent needs to do is to take on the character we want to be: step into his shoes, think like him, move like him, let the voice and speech respond to the thoughts and movement. The dialogue that emerges will surprise you! Children are uncritical and will accept the imaginary character, responding in role to anyone, or anything, we play. If I put on a hat and introduce myself as a policeman, a pirate, or a shopkeeper, the offer is accepted. Equally, if I become very round and blow myself up bigger and bigger, I'm a balloon or a washing machine or a dinosaur.

The teacher's role is crucial to drama for the children under five who need us to guide, lead, and initiate the action. Once the class is engaged, the teacher can move in and out as necessary, standing aside at times when children are involved in the role-play, stepping back in to suggest a way out, change location, or move the action along.

Unlocking imagination

An easy way in is through stories:

■ We can maximize the drama when we read a book, bringing it alive through imagination and voice. Take time to let the voice respond to each new character's thoughts, feelings, and movement so the vocal tone, color, and expression changes for each.

■ Extend stories by acting out the plot with the teacher as narrator and the children playing the characters, using their own words. Well-known stories like *The Three Little Pigs* and *The Three Billy Goats Gruff* work well. There's no reason why the whole class can't be the billy goats (*The Twelve Billy-Goats Gruff!*) to the teacher's troll.

■ What happens first, or next? How do the three bears make the porridge? Where do they go on their walk? What do they do? Accept contributions that are completely original, even whacky, because a child's imagination is far greater than our own.

■ Use props, masks, and suggestions of costume to aid entry into roles, but don't feel they're necessary. Costumes, too, can be imaginary. Take time to put on an imaginary hat, pick up a pair of binoculars, step into a pair of boots.

Enjoying poetry

Action rhymes that get everyone moving and joining in provide a good springboard for class activity. Poetry and good verse help students to sense the music of speech as well as to practice spontaneous vocal and physical expression. Try:

Five little squirrels
Sat up in a tree,

The first one said,
"What do I see?"

The second one said,
"A man and his son!"

The third one said,
"Then we'd better run!"

The fourth one said,
"Let's hide in the shade."

The fifth one said,
"I'm not afraid!"

Then "Boo!" said the son,
And how they did run!

■ PRESENT poems by saying them for the group, along with the actions.

■ CLARIFY that everyone has understood the meaning by talking about them and asking questions.

■ REPEAT the rhyme with everyone joining in with the words and the actions. It's important for the teacher to provide a strong lead for the children to follow. They will join in with you without thinking about it, saying the whole poem together, peering to see what the first squirrel sees, running away, and responding to the loud "Boo!" at the end.

■ EXTEND the poem through drama. Can we say it, and act it, in different ways? Feeling frightened? Feeling brave? What are the squirrels doing before the poem starts? After? Can we set the poem in the middle of a dramatic story?

This Little Puffin (New York: Penguin Books, 1991) is a marvelous teaching resource full of action rhymes to get the class excited about using voice, movement, and drama.

Children remember most of the words of a poem introduced through the PRESENT, CLARIFY, REPEAT, EXTEND method because they've absorbed it through their senses. Whether they are primarily visual, auditory, or kinesthetic learners, this method allows maximum retention. And they'll love it and want to do it again:

■ STEP 1
Present, clarify, repeat, extend in class.

■ STEP 2
Give each child a copy to take home. Would they like to share it with mummy?

■ STEP 3
Make squirrel masks for drama.

■ STEP 4
Do it again in class, wearing our masks.

■ STEP 5
Would anyone like to say the words of one of the squirrels in our drama?

■ STEP 6
Would anyone like to try to say the whole poem on their own?

Children are not threatened by questions asked in role. If the teacher, as "Chief Squirrel," asks for help from the group it's given freely and confidently. When "The ShopKeeper" asks "The Customer" what she'd like, the child, in role, practises a life skill she will in time use assertively outside class. Communication skills develop in this way: if "Squirrel" can do it, so can I.

Most students memorize poems and are comfortable standing up in front of the group to present them in their own individual way. Further, you'll hear in their confident voices that they have picked up the rhythm and melody of the language, the dynamics of the words, grammar, and a wide range of vocal expression.

Playing with puppets

There is a very special magic in puppets! A puppet is a little like a mask: the wearer brings the puppet alive and it, in turn, enables the wearer to take on the role. Even the shyest child feels comfortable speaking to, or through, a puppet. Our children chat through their puppets, watch puppet shows, hug and talk to the puppets afterwards, perform their own shows, and enable their puppets to say tongue twisters and speech exercises.

Making music and singing songs

Songs enable us to absorb vocabulary, rhythm, and structure of language. Consider how many songs you know all the words to — without even trying to learn them. Dramatic songs that encourage movement are a marvelous source of language to use with the PRESENT, CLARIFY, REPEAT, EXTEND method.

Music is the fastest route to the imagination so we use plenty of it in our early childhood programs, including recorded music to stimulate movement, percussion instruments for establishing a beat, and a keyboard to synthesise atmospheric sound. It's easy to focus group attention using sound and to create the mood of a cool forest, a gloomy cave, or a fairground full of fun.

What other equipment do I need?

The most useful tool is a props box, full of unusual odds and ends that stimulate ideas. The best costumes for drama leave everything open to the imagination — a piece of cloth is better than an expensive cape because it can double as a blanket, a shawl, a robe, a bundle, a tent, the sea, the wind, or at least 50 other vital ingredients for an adventure. Never throw anything out! There's a role for old credit cards, computer keyboards, bags of all descriptions, hats and other headgear. You'll find a torch, a telephone, a variety of cloths in different textures, assorted boxes, and jewelry to be invaluable treasures. The only real essential for creating drama is you — along with your imagination and desire to learn with (and from!) your students.

Julia Gabriel is founder and principal of Julia Gabriel Speech and Drama Center, in Singapore and London, and Chiltern House Child-Care. Based in Singapore she has spent almost 20 years teaching communication programs using drama. For her services to speech and drama, Julia was awarded honorary life membership of Guildhall School of Music and Drama, by the Corporation of London, in 1995.

Using Beginnings Workshop to Train Teachers by Kay Albrecht

Reflection: Ask teachers to reflect on their early childhood creative drama memories. Do they remember feeling like the little girl described by Leithold? Do they recall a teacher who incorporated creative drama in their classroom?

Getting Started: Break the ice with a rousing round of "If You're Happy and You Know It" as described by Leithold (p. 85). Ask teachers to identify feelings from their daily experiences in the classroom to include in the song (like joy, confusion, excitement, fatigue, etc.) Or use Stotter's Mood Game (p. 79) as an opening activity, perhaps sending the director out first!

Exploring Ideas: Divide teachers into pairs. Brainstorm possible roles that each teacher might incorporate into his or her teaching repertoire. The role could be a character (like He Who Must Be Obeyed or Old Mother Hubbard), an animal, insect, or creature (like a firefly, tiger, or dinosaur), or even a personality (like Mr. Green Jeans or Mother Goose). Have some fun with this step! Take the time to describe and expand the role, the name of the character, and the personality it might have.

Dressing the Part: Help teachers further flesh out their roles. Provide markers, paper, crayons, watercolors, and collage materials for teachers to illustrate their ideas. Share the illustrations. Then make plans to collect the materials and props to support the role they have identified. If the workshop format is being used, it will be necessary to provide props and supports for teachers to select from to dress for the role developed.

Cueing the Crowd: Explore with teachers how children will know when the teacher is in the new creative drama role. Is there a special cue like putting on a hat or tying on an apron? Or perhaps use a special transition activity like turning your back to the children only to reappear in the new role. Brainstorm other ideas to help teachers adopt the role and help children know the teacher has assumed the role.

Present, Clarify, Repeat, Extend: Give teachers a creative drama assignment. They must use the role they created in **Dressing the Part** to plan and implement a creative drama activity using Gabriel's four-step process (see p. 72). Suggestions and ideas are readily available in Stotter's, Leithold's, and Gabriel's articles. Ask teachers to demonstrate their activity to others at the next meeting. Encourage them to try out the idea with children in their classrooms before the next meeting.

Sharing Experiences: Share experiences. Ask each teacher to give a creative drama demonstration using what she has learned in the workshop or staff meeting series. Celebrate the drama demonstrations with lots of applause and bravos.

Parent Newsletter: Discuss introducing how children learn from creative dramatics in your school newsletter. List topics that might be included and assign articles to interested teachers. Make a list of sample activities to share with parents, perhaps using some of the great ideas developed by teachers!

Glossary: Create a glossary to support this *Beginnings Workshop*. Include words like paralanguage, communication support, stage presence, vocal pitch.

Exchange Resources for Teachers on Creative Drama

"Developing a storytelling culture in our programs." Margie Carter, January/February 1997 (Issue #113).

"The value of fairy and folk tales." Beginning Workshop, July/August, 1992 (Issue #86).

CREATIVE DRAMATICS

Fairy Tales Enhance Imagination and Creative Thinking

by Olga Sidlovskaya

Early childhood is the age of fairy tales. Language used in fairy tales is uncomplicated and doesn't exceed a child's comprehension capabilities. Any fairy tale is, by definition, simple yet mysterious. Hardly does one begin the narration with "Once upon a time . . . " that children calm down and are carried away into the world of their fantasies. Fairy tales support the development of imagination and creative thinking, one of the fundamental psychological formations of the pre-school childhood. The imagination of a child is the soil from which sprouts and grows to perfection a scientist, an inventor, an artist.

Fairy tales are one of the best means of developing this important psychological process of the early childhood — imagination. The style of a fairy tale is easy to understand for a child. Children cannot reason logically at this age, and fairy tales do not overburden them with logic. No child likes to be instructed directly, and fairy tales never teach children in this way. At most, fairy tales hint at what would be the best thing to do in this or that situation.

Fairy tales set forth and help to resolve moral problems. Most children identify with positive characters; fairy tales teach kindness and virtue and they nurture such faculties in a child. Every fairy tale proves that it is best to be good.

When reading or reciting fairy tales to a child, we introduce her to the world of coded situations and problems, to the world of experience, enigmas, and mystery. Imagination development necessitates enriching sensory experience. The more a child hears, sees, and experiences, the more she knows and acquires. This means that she possesses more elements of reality in her experience, and so her imagination is considerably more productive and much more active.

Yet the environment of a fairy tale is not enough for developing imagination, for how the narration is presented is extremely important to how it is perceived and comprehended. This is where adults step in — psychologists, parents, teachers, and other people responsible for the upbringing and development of any given child. During this period, when representational thinking is rapidly developing, the material needs to be presented so that the child can see the action of a fairy tale in its most vivid, representational way. Television and theatre are not the only means of acquiring such experience; one can play the plot out, live through it. Role playing should be arranged so that all senses are activated.

When we started fairy tale therapy, we noted that children are not moved by the stories deeply enough after merely reading to them. It is difficult for them to reconstruct such details of the plot as landscapes or the kind of nature presented. Children do not easily imagine either the forest that Ivan the Prince goes through or the place where the magic oak grows. Illustrations help, but not every book has them and not every episode of narration is accompanied with pictures. We decided to draw with children, restoring all the episodes after having read them, and we saw that every child perceives fairy tales differently. Drawing helped children to like the story better and to immerse themselves more deeply in the action. Also, their own drawings helped them to recite the tale later on.

Then, as the next stage, children constructed the landscape of a fairy tale on the floor with the help of multi-coloured, differently-shaped forms, both big and small, and with various fabrics of different textures. "Ivan the Prince went into the fields," said the story, and we spread fabrics with daisies and cornflowers on the floor. We built the forest that Little Red Riding Hood went through with fabrics. In that forest (which consisted of a number of fabrics of different hues of green), there was also a creek (a long light blue strip of chiffon) and a meadow with poppies (chinz fabric with the printings of big poppies on it).

Later, when we played out the fairy tale, Red Riding Hood *listened* to birds singing in the forest, she *picked* poppies, *washed* her face in the stream. Building fairy tale landscapes assists children in grasping the meaning, and it prompts deeper understanding of the characters. We always stress the necessity of telling children about the nature of the country from where the fairy tale came, about the place where its authors lived. If it is a Japanese fairy tale, we talk about Japan, if it is "Little Red Riding Hood," we tell about the nature of France. Introducing children to the culture of the tale helps them to understand that every nation has its own fairy tales and that the names of heroes are not the only thing that makes them different.

Also, we tell fairy tales with the help of small pieces of fabric. We model the story. Fabrics of different textures and colours are used, such as those found in abundance at everyone's house. As the tale is being told, children relate its characters to fabric pieces. In the beginning of the narration, a child can associate the Prince with a piece of blue velvet and lay the piece out on the table in front of him. As the narration goes on, the child continues to lay out pieces, ssociating them with landscapes, heroes, magical objects, and so on. It is worth mentioning that toward the end of the fairy tale the same Prince can be associated by the same child with the golden, glittering, or brocade fabric. It is important that such changes help us as adults to track changes in the child's perception of a fairy tale, as well as to compare his perception with ours. This is very important.

The next stage is to *live through* the tale using the sense of smell. When asked, children showed that their knowledge of smells is insufficient. Some children seemed to be surprised when they heard that everything around them smells differently. We made a collection of smells. We put different herbs and objects that have a definite smell into photo film containers. We collected mostly objects that have a strong or definite smell: cinnamon, cardamom, nutmeg, walnut, mustard, bay leaves, sweet peas, tarragon, horseradish, mint , different kinds of fruit and vegetables, wood, metal objects (paper clips, nails), newspapers, perfumes of different types, orange and lemon peelings, iodine, sunflower oil, honey, vanilla, tea, coffee, cocoa, dry milk, and others.

When reading or telling a fairy tale, the first assignment is to select smells or scents that can be associated with the characters. It can be a single sample or a whole collection of scents. For this purpose, we specifically use tubs to be used as containers for any given combination. For instance, *a forest smell* is always complex and combined. In this case children put perfume fragrances together with the samples of forest plants, mushrooms, trees, and flowers. They enjoy selecting the *right* sample.

Next we make compositions representing the smell of the location where the action takes place — a house, a room, a castle). This kind of activity adds to the experience of a fairy tale; it deepens and broadens it.

To answer the question of how it smells inside the hen-legged hut, children have to decide together what smells could be associated with the interiors of Baba Yoga's hut. By doing this, children learn to reason, to consider such important details as features, peculiarities, and eccentricities of the characters, which is of great help in developing their imagination and creativity.

We use noises and sounds for the same purpose. We have collections of bells, drums, and rattles, as well as various jars filled with small objects, which when shaken make various sounds and noises. Jars can be filled with dry peas, millet, semolina, water, broken egg shells, dry orange peelings, metal shavings, and so on. To make noises and sounds, we use voice as well. For example, when depicting noises of a forest, some children wave fabrics, some pour water from one glass to another, others imitate the cooing of a dove, and someone can be slowly shaking a jar with buckwheat. Isn't this product of imagination wonderful? We often accompany this activity with environmental soundtracks of nature such as forests and water. Another device that we use is to have some children close their eyes and listen to the noises that other children are creating, and later everybody makes a sketch of what they imagined when listening.

Children's creativity and imagination is also developed when thinking about and making the costumes of a fairy tale character. We do not sew costumes, we combine them using the collection of fabrics of different size, colour, and texture. A child of either sex enjoys dressing up — everyone enjoys the activity. When children choose the fabric strip they think can be associated with their character, they wrap it around themselves. The task of an adult in this activity is to direct and help the child.

After children finish making their costumes, they have fun in front of the mirror, looking at themselves and each other. Then we start thinking out each character's dance. Music for the dance is chosen together, although the dance should be spontaneous. When the playback starts, the child comes out to the middle and starts dancing. When he is about to finish this improvised dance, others are invited to join in. Children surround the dancer in a circle and repeat the moves. This allows each child to perform the dance of every fairy tale character.

Thus, with the help of these diverse activities — nature presentation, costume making, dances, smell collections, sounds, and music — children are actively learning to understand the world of any given fairy tale, as well as the world of magic generally, through creative experience. They come to see fairy tale characters more clearly, they sympathise with their feelings on a deeper level, they become acquainted with the rich and diverse object world of the country in the fairy tale. Adults witness the fantastic landscape of the tale as it was made by children themselves. Children can switch roles easily because costumes are not made specifically for one person and they can be thought out in the process, as the tale is being staged.

As this improvised performance unfolds in front of the viewers, the smells which children associate with certain episodes are offered to the public. For example, when the Princess makes her appearance, a tub with various fragrances is carried out. Or when the mouse is cooking dinner in her hut, one can sense the smells of vegetables and herbs. Also, the entrance of each character is accompanied by music and dancing. All of this creates that unforgettable atmosphere of a fairy tale which thrills children.

During these activities, a child's imagination and creativity improve, as she creates and constructs the tale independently. Children enjoy showing this kind of independence. It is in the free activity that children start composing and taking part in tales.

Thinking out fairy tale plots should be initially supervised by adults. Preschoolers enjoy creating the end of the tale, making their own interpretation of the story, the beginning of which was given to them. Especially appealing to them is the opportunity to play the magician. When they work on the continuation of the story, they say *magic words* that transform them into wizards. We explain to them that this role is given to them only for a certain time, until the bell rings, after which all the players will turn back into themselves. We use a timer which is well hidden from the players. When it is time to finish, it suddenly gives a signal and children take it for a *magic bell*.

In our fairy tale therapy room, there is the wizard's throne — a chair covered with beautiful fabrics — and his robe; the fabric is chosen by children. Here we start creating a fairy tale. Whose turn it is to play is defined by throwing lots or as children wish, which is slightly more difficult for pre-schoolers. Children seat themselves in the magic chair, and taking on their image, begin the narration. It goes on until that person's imagination is exhausted. Then his place is taken by another. Everything is taped, and later the text is edited and read aloud, so that children can hear the story as outsiders. This version is also played out.

Fairy tales serve as the wrapping paper for various, even most well-known psychological methods and devices. In spite of the impressive technological progress which takes the rationalisation of our life to the limit, both children and adults are drawn to another magical world, to the world of a fairy tale where the riches of the national experience are enclosed. This should not surprise us, for fairy tales are the treasury of human relationships; they not only stir our imagination and help us to create, they also charge our lives with positive emotions, they unite different nations and generations. So let fairy tales help everybody, both the little ones and adults, both children and their parents, to enjoy life, to smile more often, to feel happy because we have touched the world of open-mindedness and purity.

Olga Sidlovskaya is the supervising professor of the faculty of pre-school education of Karelia State Pedagogical University in Russia and a psychologist practising methods and devices of fairy tale art therapy with children, teenagers, and adults. She is also experienced in working with children with health problems and social needs.

Using Beginnings Workshop to Train Teachers of Preschoolers and School-Agers
by Kay Albrecht

Sidlovskaya describes a psychological therapeutic approach for using fairy tales with children. Teachers are not therapists, but they can use many of the techniques Sidlovskaya explains in educational form.

Add the Nose: Brainstorm ways to add scents and aroma to creative drama activities. Make a list of fragrances that can be put in scent jars to enhance tales. Ask for a volunteer to prepare the scent jars and add them to the props teachers may use for creative drama.

What Do You Hear: Brainstorm sound makers that could be added to prop boxes for enhancing creative drama activities. Ask for a volunteer to collect some of the sound makers you identify.

CREATIVE DRAMATICS

Starting With A Story

by Ruth Stotter

"Once upon a time. . . ." "In the beginning. . . ." It takes only a few words to be transported to the magical world of story. Traditional storytelling has been called "theatre of the mind" — each audience member pictures in his or her own imagination the story's characters, scenery, objects, and action.

Storytelling can be an ideal strategy to introduce creative dramatics. It helps, of course, if the stories have engaging story lines, interesting characters, humor, and suspense. Engaged in this playful, non-judgmental activity, children will experiment playing the roles of animals and people by changing their vocal pitch, facial expression, body language, and even by creating original dialogue.

When you incorporate storytelling and creative drama, you are helping children:

■ Have opportunities to express themselves orally
■ Learn to convey a sequence of events
■ Learn to organize and express ideas clearly
■ Gain experience in retaining information
■ Develop a sense of playing to an audience
■ Learn to appreciate word choice and styles of communication
■ Gain self-esteem; storytelling is a legitimate way to be looked at and listened to
■ Learn basic acting skills
■ Work with entertaining texts that have the potential to enhance understanding of other lifestyles and world views
■ Escape to the land of enchantment and adventure
■ Have fun

Before introducing stories for the children to enact, I recommend beginning with a few simple games and exercises to stimulate creativity and to build performance confidence. Here are six suggested activities.

ACTIVITY ONE — Participation stories

With younger children, stories with chants and sound effects encourage audience participation. Elicit their participation as an organic part of the story rather than as a stated manipulative directive. For example, instead of saying, "Every time I say "cat," you say "meow," say something like, "The cat was angry. And an angry cat says . . . (put your hand on your ear and lean forward — they will respond without your having to tell them what to say).

Try having the children say the story character's dialogue together. For example, in the well-known folk tale "The Little Red Hen," the entire class can answer together as the Dog, Cat, and Sheep when they reply, "Not I" and at the end when they say, "I will help you eat the bread." Or, you might divide the group up into sections — each section saying one animal's lines. The group can also say the Little Red Hen's repeated line, "Then I will do it all by myself."

Even very young children can add personality to these animals if you describe the animals by saying, "The lazy dog answered . . . ; the conceited, arrogant cat answered . . . ; the busy, pre-occupied sheep answered. . . ."

Here are a few excellent stories that incorporate audience participation:

1. *Iroko Man: A Yoruba Folktale* retold by Phyllis Gershator (New York: Orchard Books, 1994).

2. "Coyote's Rain Song" from *Twenty Tellable Tales: Audience Participation Folktales for the Beginning Storyteller* by Margaret Read MacDonald (New York: H. W. Wilson, 1986).

3. *Squeaky Door: A Folktale from Puerto Rico* by Laura Simms (New York: Crown Publishers, 1990).

4. "Lion and Rabbit" from *Joining In: An Anthology of Participation Stories and How to Tell Them.* Compiled by Teresa Miller with assistance from Anne Pellowski. Edited by Norma Livo (Cambridge, MA: Yellow Moon Press, 3rd printing, 1990).

5. "Princess and the Ogre" from *Joining In* (see #4 above).

6. "Agaboogawa" from *Joining In* (see #4 above).

7. *Jack Always Seeks His Fortune* by Donald Davis (Little Rock, AR: August House, 1992).

ACTIVITY TWO — Story: Turtle's Tale

A turtle is walking down the road and meets a cat who says, "Turtle, it is going to rain. You better go home." Turtle replies, "Thank you very much." Then Turtle meets a dog who says, "Turtle, it is going to rain. You better go home." Turtle replies, "Thank you very much. " Then turtle meets a sheep who says, "Turtle, it is going to rain. You better go home." Turtle replies, "Thank you very much." Just then it begins to rain. Turtle pulls in his front legs, pulls in his back legs, and pulls in his head. Turtle is home — safe and dry!

> — *Told to me by a school child in Honolulu, Hawaii*

Ask the children, "Why would Cat tell Turtle that it is going to rain and that he should go home?" Perhaps they will say, "Because Cat is bossy." Or, "Because Cat cares about Turtle." Or, "Because Cat is afraid of the water and thinks Turtle will be, too." Select an answer and say, "Yes. So, how would a bossy, or a caring, or a frightened cat say that line — *Turtle, it is going to rain. You had better go home?*" Repeat this process with each animal, giving them a motivation for telling Turtle what to do.

Would Turtle answer in a different tone of voice when he says, "Thank you very much" to a bossy cat? A caring cat? A frightened cat? In this way, as with "The Little Red Hen," you are demonstrating that they can create personalities, moods, and idiosyncrasies for story characters which will enhance the telling.

After you tell the story as a group, with all the children playing all the animals, ask for four volunteers to act out the story. Or, divide the class into groups of four and let each group take turns performing their version. Allow rehearsal time.

ACTIVITY THREE — Sound effects

Sound effects add fun and excitement to story enactments. Here are a few sound effects to have students practice. These can be done with the class as a whole, or as an activity in groups of two or three with the rest of the class guessing what sound effect is being communicated.

DOOR SLAM
Ordinary door in a house.
Try a door slam for a mouse house.
Try a door slam for a large castle.
Add a lock after you close the door.

ZOOMING CARS AND HORNS
"Jooom" "jooom" while turning your head may work.
"Beeep" "beeep" in nasal voice may work.

ANIMAL DRINKING WATER

BIRDS SINGING IN A FOREST
Try a series of three bird-like sounds . . . rotate them a few times so that we clearly hear three different kinds of birds.

BIRDS FLYING BY
Start softly, get louder, then softer.

WAVES CRASHING ON THE BEACH

DUCK FAMILY
Father duck. Mother duck. Baby duck.

NORTH WIND

STARS
Create a sound for each little star popping out in the night sky.

PIANO
Pink-a-pink-a-pink-a-pink, pink-pink or whatever you can come up with.

BANJO OR GUITAR OR UKULELE

DRUM

ACTIVITY FOUR — Mood game

Tell the class that while one person leaves the room, the group will select a mood that they will all enact. When this person comes back, he or she will ask three to five children a question, which will be answered in the selected mood. With very young children, or with a small group, you may prefer that everyone has an opportunity. Encourage questions that cannot be answered with a simple yes or no. Instead of, "Do you like ice cream?" ask, "What are your favorite desserts?"

Mood Game — Level Two for School-agers
The group selects both a character and a mood. So, for example, the group will all be fussy, faultfinding cats; or fussy, faultfinding giants; or fussy, faultfinding princesses; or fussy, faultfinding mice. This time, the person who has left the room tries to guess both the character and the mood.

ACTIVITY FIVE —
Developing instant stage presence

Ask each child, one at a time, to come up and stand before the group. Model this as you explain the directions. Balance your weight evenly on both feet, making sure your knees are not locked. Look around the class and make eye contact with a few people. Smile. Then say, "I like pizza with (add an ingredient)." Each child has to use a different ingredient, one that has not already been stated. As soon as he or she finishes this sentence, the group applauds. The speaker must remain standing until the applause quiets down before returning to his or her seat. This bonds the audience and performer. Furthermore, walking away while the audience is still clapping communicates a lack of humility and appreciation for their applause. I have found that this simple exercise gives even very young students confidence and stage presence.

ACTIVITY SIX — Liar's club for school-agers

The goal is to sound logical and convincing. Each child creates a use or explanation for an object that is passed around the circle. So, for example, if a paper clip is being passed around one student might say, "Oh, this is wonderful! This is a tool used by astronauts to measure distance. They use this section to examine nearby planets, and the lower section to study the earth." Next child: "Oh no, you are wrong. This is a device to clean horse hooves when they get small pebbles and mud." Next child, "You both have good imaginations, but I will tell you what this actually is. I see this used all the time at the cooking school to separate the egg white from the yolk."

I like to do this exercise with small circles of six to ten students. If the object is passed around the circle a second time, the explanations and definitions become increasingly imaginative.

Remember, there is no right way to tell a story. Most of all, you want it to be a positive experience. I hope that you will enjoy using storytelling and these activities as an approach to creative drama!

Recommended for your library

Hamilton, M., & Weiss, M. (1996). *Stories in my pocket: Tales kids can tell.* Golden, CO: Fulcrum Publishing.

Lipman, D. (1995). *Storytelling games.* Phoenix, AZ: Oryx Press.

Miller, T. (1990). *Joining in: An anthology of participation stories and how to tell them.* Cambridge, MA: Yellow Moon Press.

Livo, N. J., & Rietz, S. A. (1987). *Storytelling activities.* Littleton, CO: Libraries Unlimited, Inc.

MacDonald, M. R. (1986). *Twenty tellable tales: Audience participation folktales for the beginning storyteller.* New York: H. W. Wilson Company.

Pellowski, A. (1987). *The family storytelling handbook.* New York: Macmillan Publishing Company.

Stern, A. (1995). *World folktales: An anthology of multicultural folk literature.* Lincolnwood, IL: National Textbook Company.

Stotter, R. (1999). *The golden axe.* Contains 33 full texts of the same story tale type from around the world and three scripts ready to use for play acting, puppetry, or reader's theatre. There are also interpretive notes for each story and tips for story-telling. Stinson Beach: Stotter Press (available from Baker & Taylor, Barnes & Noble, and Amazon.com).

Ruth Stotter is a storyteller and folklorist who has received numerous awards, authored several publications encouraging the art of storytelling, and is currently the Consultant on Storytelling for the Puppeteers of America.

CREATIVE DRAMATICS

Using Creative Dramatics to Include All Children

by Kirsten Haugen

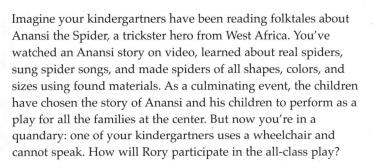

Imagine your kindergartners have been reading folktales about Anansi the Spider, a trickster hero from West Africa. You've watched an Anansi story on video, learned about real spiders, sung spider songs, and made spiders of all shapes, colors, and sizes using found materials. As a culminating event, the children have chosen the story of Anansi and his children to perform as a play for all the families at the center. But now you're in a quandary: one of your kindergartners uses a wheelchair and cannot speak. How will Rory participate in the all-class play?

Prepare an accessible environment

As you create opportunities for creative dramatics in your program, the thoughtfulness you put into accommodating children with disabilities will benefit all the children.

■ **Gross motor support.** Provide stable furnishings that won't tip and sufficient space without obstacles. Children can often use scooter boards, adapted tricycles, and pedal cars as alternative ways to get around. Consult a physical therapist beforehand if you want a child with physical disabilities to "try new things."

■ **Fine motor support.** Include costumes and props that are simpler to use; try large knobs, handles and switches, and easy-to-fasten alternatives to buttons. Lightweight props can be made of Styrofoamô. Also available are battery-operated puppet stands that spin or rock with the touch of a switch.

■ **Visual support.** Help children with visual impairments know when, where, and how to participate by giving hands-on narrated "tours" of objects in the environment beforehand, and provide an ongoing commentary during activities. Keep the environment organized, use high contrasts in colors and textures, and provide good lighting, so children with poor vision can easily find things.

■ **Communication support.** Provide rich photos and pictures to spark ideas for dramatic play; put the pictures in "windows" with curtains to lift and peek; label the environment with words, words, words. When you speak, remember to face children with hearing impairments or auditory processing difficulties. Incorporate sign language and captioned pictures into songs and games. Consider adapted tape recorders, talking photo frames, or special voice output devices that play back one or more messages which a peer can record beforehand.

■ **Behavioral support.** Keep background noise and distractions to a minimum; work in smaller groups; preteach challenging skills in a step-by-step fashion; allow for breaks from a group activity.

■ **Creative costuming.** Special equipment can be a bonus rather than a burden — use cardboard, poster paint, and imagination to build a bus, a bulldozer, or a bakery right around a child's wheelchair.

Support participation

Welcome diversity in terms of how children perceive of and participate in creative dramatics. Creative dramatics can include speaking, dancing, singing, playing instruments, providing sound effects, pantomime, puppetry, creating sets, costumes and scenery, operating curtains, controlling lights, designing programs, and more. If you put on a performance, be sure to acknowledge all forms of participation equally. In addition, try these specific strategies to enable all children to participate:

■ Observe how each child participates in free play and other activities so you can provide dramatic roles that match their skills and interests.

■ Trust your own imagination and creativity . . . and ask other teachers and parents for ideas.

■ Ask the children to brainstorm ideas and strategies. Children often come up with unique and practical solutions for including their peers in all kinds of activities.

■ Teach children with special needs a new story, activity, or skill beforehand so they are already "experts" when the whole group joins in.

■ Provide partners. Match children with different skills so that together they can accomplish a task. One child can move the puppet while the other speaks the lines.

■ Sometimes a child's special equipment can provide unique opportunities for roles, costumes, etc.

■ Provide ample time to prepare, explore, and practice. Your first attempts to include a child with differences may not work as planned, or a child with special needs may need additional exposure to materials and activities.

■ Above all, have fun with the "fuzzy lines" between drama, pretend play, art, dance, literature, block play, and more.

"People First" language and images

You can include children with disabilities in creative dramatics, portray characters with disabilities in your dramatic productions (and in books, posters, etc.), use creative dramatics to stimulate thinking about people with disabilities, and provide dolls or props such as wheelchairs, mobility canes, or braces in your dramatic play areas. It is important in each case that you model positive, appropriate language and images about people with disabilities.

■ Emphasize people first, disabilities second. Say "a child with Down syndrome" or "a teacher with cerebral palsy" instead of "a Down child" or "a palsied teacher."

■ Emphasize abilities. Say "Becky uses a wheelchair," instead of "Becky is confined to a wheelchair."

■ Emphasize practical needs instead of stereotypes. Say "Brian is blind, so he's had to learn how to pay extra attention to where sounds come from" instead of "Blind people have such a special sense of hearing."

■ Answer questions about disabilities directly and honestly, in positive and practical terms. "No, Emily can't talk yet, but have you noticed how she looks at you and then at what she wants, and smiles or frowns to tell you how she feels?"

■ Portray people with disabilities in active, leadership positions rather than passive roles. You need not look far — people with disabilities run companies and non-profits, play sports, work in universities and research facilities, and perform in dance companies and theater troupes.

■ Learn from your children. I once overheard a kindergartner say, "Hey Jen, I'll push your wheelchair if you carry my library books."

Back to Rory and the class play

Now it's time to think how you might include Rory in the class play. Will he sit in the audience, or will he operate the lights or music? Hold up posters to go with the narration? Speak his lines using a voice output device? Play his part with an adapted puppet? Use his power wheelchair to move sets across the stage? Once you begin to imagine the possibilities, the challenge may come down to which role to choose.

Resources for including children with disabilities in creative dramatics

Accessible Arts newsletter — available from 1100 State Avenue, Kansas City, KS 66102-4411, (913) 281-1133, fax (913) 281-1515, e-mail: accarts@hotmail.com.

Americans for the Arts provides links to web sites on the arts for children birth to age 8 — 1000 Vermont Avenue NW, 12th floor, Washington, DC 20005, (202) 371-2830, fax (202) 371-0424, www.artsusa.org.

AssisTech, Inc. makes adapted puppetry stands and related materials — PO Box 137, Stow, NY 14785, (888) ASISTEK, (716) 789-4197, fax (716) 789-4644, www.assisttech.com.

The Bridge School's web site has creative ideas and instructions for costumes for kids who use wheelchairs — 545 Eucalyptus Avenue, Hillsborough, CA 94010, (650) 696-7295, www.bridgeschool.org/about/about_halloween.html.

Creative Communicating provides story-time ideas to encourage participation, language, and literacy in children with developmental delays and language disabilities — PO Box 3358, Park City, UT 84060, (435) 645-7737, fax (435) 658-0925, www.creative-comm.com.

Linda J. Burkhart shows how to make a communication device from a talking photo frame — 6201 Candle Court, Eldersburg, MD 21784, (410) 795-4561, www.lburkhart.com/pframe.htm.

Toys for Special Children provides simple voice output devices, ability switches, adapted toys, musical instruments, and more — 385 Warburton Avenue, Hastings-on-Hudson, NY 10706, (800) 832-8697, (914) 478-0960, fax (914) 478-7030, www.enablingdevices.com.

Special thanks to Brigitte Galvan, The Bridge School, Alice Wershing,
and Susan Thiele.

Kirsten lives with her husband Dennis Galvan and their two sons in Eugene, Oregon. When she is not immersed in the joys and challenges of parenting, Kirsten works as a consultant for educational and assistive technology, developing inclusive, creative learning and play strategies for children with and without disabilities, in early childhood and elementary settings.

Using Beginnings Workshop to Train Teachers of Preschoolers and School-Agers
by Kay Albrecht

Practicing Emphasizing People, Abilities, and Practical Needs First: Haugen's wonderful proposal to emphasize people, abilities, and practical needs can be just the tool sensitive teachers are searching for. But, for most of us, it takes practice to be comfortable with using the right words. Create a practice session to work on describing children, both with and without special needs, using Haugen's suggestions. Ask teachers to write down descriptions of children in their classrooms. Then use the three guidelines to assess whether the description focuses on people, abilities, and practical needs first. If not, discuss how to modify the descriptions.

Talking About Differences: Continue this practice session by exploring how to talk about differences. Role play ways to describe differences between children, focusing on using words to point out practical, compensating strategies that children can use with each other.

CREATIVE DRAMATICS

Helping Teachers Become Comfortable With Creative Dramatics

by Naomi Leithold

Terri stares into the sea of eager eyes. As she stands there trembling, her palms sweat and her heart flutters. Her legs feels like lead. Will words come out of her mouth when she opens it? Will her legs ever move again?

She keeps reassuring herself that she isn't performing before thousands of people at The Kennedy Center. Those eyes belong to a group of preschoolers, children whom she adores and plays with on a daily basis. Yet, when she tries to do creative dramatics with them, her mind transforms them into an audience of discerning critics.

After several uncomfortable attempts presenting dramatic activities, Terri decides that these anxiety-producing lessons are not essential. After all, dramatics are just an extra frill in the early childhood curriculum. She already provides a variety of more important developmental experiences. And the anxiety it causes her isn't going to make her a better teacher.

Terri may feel that she's reached some logical conclusions, but her conclusions aren't necessarily correct. Dramatics and its benefits can be an important part of the early childhood curriculum, and teaching it does not have to produce cold sweats. There are many fun and imaginative creative dramatic lessons that don't require a high level of risk taking — activities that both timid teachers and students will enjoy. Through these experiences, many important early childhood skills will be developed in ways that are not possible with other activities.

Learning experiences for children

Helping children to build a positive self-concept is an important goal of any early childhood program. Body awareness, an understanding of how the body works, and comfort in moving your body are integral parts of a good self-image. Dramatic representation requires children to control their bodies, twisting and turning, to become something or someone else. As they take on these new roles, they are able to express themselves through both nonverbal and verbal communication. This additional mode of communication is often helpful for young children who tend to be more physical in their approach to life.

Creative dramatic activities don't require a specific outcome. Each child can be encouraged to use his creativity to the maximum; individuality is accepted. Children become less self-conscious and more willing to share their ideas with others.

Dramatic experiences offer another method for teaching early childhood concepts. Opposites, feelings, animals, movements, and modes of transportation are a few of the themes that can easily be introduced through creative dramatics. Pre-literacy skills are also greatly augmented by dramatic representation. When a story from a book or a story authored by a child is acted out, reading takes on a new meaning. Physical movement brings objects into a different dimension, one that is more easily understood by young children, who tend to be concrete in their thinking. Nonverbal communication also bridges the language barrier. Balls bounce up and down, no matter what language you are speaking. This additional learning tool is an advantage for meeting the differing needs and learning styles of all children.

Taking the first steps

Are these many benefits of creative dramatics compelling enough for those of you who are still trembling? Where do you start? How do you stop trembling? The best place to start is by looking at this in the proper perspective. Put yourself in the children's shoes. They are just as unsure of themselves as you are. Creative dramatics is new and intimidating to them also. They, too, will be inhibited when asked to create dramatic representations. They, too, will be fearful of making mistakes when trying something new, especially when they feel all eyes are upon them. It might help your shaking knees if you look at this as an experience that you are sharing. Here are a few guidelines that will help you to choose a stress-free starting point:

■ Start Where You Are Comfortable

Early childhood creative dramatics is not a Broadway production. When you first begin, think of the activities you're doing as more closely related to creative movement than drama. Group activities — where everyone can blend into the background, including you — make everyone comfortable.

■ Introduce Uncomplicated Activities That Require Minimal Risk Taking

Remain in your chair at first and work up to whole body movements. Use activities that you are already familiar with and build upon them. Songs and finger plays that have dramatic elements are easy starting points!

■ Rely on a Helping Hand

This can come in the form of a person or a thing. Sometimes having a "partner" makes the situation less frightening and takes some of the attention away from you. The partner can be a teacher's aide, a puppet, a stuffed animal, or a prop such as an interesting hat or magic wand. These partners can be used to introduce the activity and/or do it with you.

■ Practice Where You Can Be Yourself

In the privacy of your empty bedroom or shower, let yourself go. Be silly and crazy. Look into a mirror and move your face every which way.

Of course, your inhibitions will take over once you enter your classroom, but you can slowly battle them. In the quiet of the book corner, read a book in a dramatic fashion or try a quiet dramatic activity with one child and then maybe a few more. Once you get positive feedback from your students, it will be much easier to continue. You will be focusing not on yourself but rather on their enjoyment and interaction.

Activities for beginning

The following is a list of activities that keep the above guidelines in mind. In no time, you will be a real pro and you will be able to think of many more on your own or with the help of the children.

■ Sing a Little Tune

The following songs lend themselves to creative dramatics. Use them as a whole classroom activity. You can start out with just hand movements and facial expressions, but then eventually move to whole body involvement.

"If You're Happy and You Know It." Act out the following emotions or state of being: sad, angry, tired, hungry. Children can suggest their own.

Change the words "Have You Ever Seen a Lassie." Children love mixing things up and here they can choose different animals or occupations to act out: *Have you ever seen an elephant go this way and that way? Go this way and that way? Have you ever seen an elephant go this way and that?*

"Eeensy, Weensy Spider." Have some fun with this childhood favorite and turn that little spider into: *the great big spider* or *the very hungry spider*, or *the very silly spider*, or *the very tired spider*. Try to reflect the meaning of the words with voice inflection.

■ Rhyme Time

Act out nursery rhymes first as a whole group, then with children taking specific parts. When given parts, small props can be used (e.g. a hat for Little Miss Muffet and a spider puppet).

■ Classroom Trips

Transitions. Take the children from one activity to another (e.g. from circle time to snack) by having them move in different ways — move as rabbits, elephants, robots, rag dolls.

Play background music. Any instrumental music such as classical, jazz, ethnic will work well. Predetermine objects or feelings that the music depicts (e.g., animal movements, wind, toy movements). Everyone moves in imitation of these objects to the beat of the music. Keep changing the kind of object, direction, and speed so the activity remains interesting. Hap Palmer has a recording, "Let's Pretend," that tells children what to pretend to be as they move to the appropriate accompanying music.

Acting around the room. Take a trip around the room acting as if you are: walking in puddles, stuck in glue, walking through mud, climbing high stairs, walking through leaves, etc. You can use a drum to keep the beat as you go. You could also use the song by Ella Jenkins, "You Walk and You Stop." Just substitute the appropriate words.

■ A Little Bit of Magic

Magic wand. Wave a magic wand over a group of children to change them into the object you call out. Wave the wand again to change them into something else.

Magic hands. How many animals (rabbit, crocodile, butterfly) can you make out of your hands?

Magic bag. Tell the children you have an imaginary magic bag and in that bag is a mask. When you put it on, your face will change. Advise them that they also have pretend magic bags in front of them. Announce what kind of mask is in the bags (happy, sad, angry, etc.). All of the bags have the same mask. Put on the mask by reaching into the bag and moving your hands down over your faces. Once your hands are past your faces, your expressions should depict the type of mask you are "wearing." This can become a guessing game with one person putting on a mask and everyone else guessing what kind is being worn. This activity is not only a lot of fun; it also helps children learn how to "read" emotions in themselves and others.

Magic door. Open up a magic door to take a walk through the seasons and pantomime while you narrate actions that are associated with each season. *Fall:* kicking leaves, jumping into piles of leaves, raking leaves, picking apples, trick-or-treating. *Winter:* dressing in winter clothes, building a snowman, drinking hot chocolate, making snow angels. *Spring:* birds singing, walking in the rain, jumping in puddles. *Summer:* swimming, playing in the playground, building a sand castle, eating corn on the cob.

Magic carpet. Take a ride. What do you see? Get off the carpet in the sky and become a bird. Float in the sky like the clouds.

Stop and freeze into a cloud shape. Have other children tell what you look like.

■ **Imagine That!**

Everyone closes their eyes and imagines various objects or situations that you describe. When you open your eyes, they become what you described. "Close your eyes and see a big round ball. Open your eyes and bounce like the ball." Ask children what color ball they are and if they are big or little. Some other possibilities are:

Eyes closed	Eyes open
A little seed	It grows
A hatching egg	It hatches
A big box	Open it and find something inside
An apple tree	Climb the tree, pick apples, and eat them

I hope that the thought of creative dramatics no longer gives you weak knees. Look at those eager eyes as partners in a playful journey. Just remember to pack your imagination and don't start by trying to climb the highest mountain. The foothills will be just fine to begin!

Naomi Leithold is a nationally acclaimed storyteller, writer, and early childhood educator who lives in the Chicago area. She can be reached by e-mail at storypol@aol.com.